Activity Book

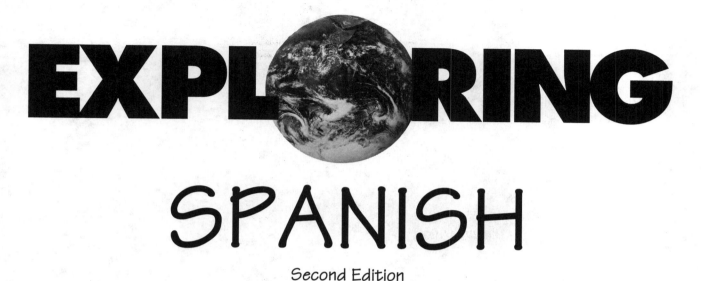

EXPLORING

SPANISH

Second Edition

Joan G. Sheeran

Consultants
Judy Gray Myrth
J. Patrick McCarthy

EMC Publishing, Saint Paul, Minnesota

ISBN 0-8219-1192-9

© 1995 by EMC Corporation

Published by EMC Publishing
300 York Avenue
St. Paul, Minnesota 55101

Printed in the United States of America
1 2 3 4 5 6 7 8 9 10 XXX 99 98 97 96 95

Unit 1

7 correct

A Match column B with column A.

A

☑ You say "good-bye" to a friend. __d__

☑ You ask a new student what his name is. __c__

☑ You say "hi" to a girl. __F__

☑ You make a mistake and you feel bad about it. __b__

☒ You wish a friend well on her English test. __e__ A

☒ You greet your neighbors as they set out for an evening at the opera.

B

a. Buena suerte.

b. Lo siento.

c. ¿Cómo te llamas?

d. Adiós, Roberto.

e. Buenas noches.

f. Hola, Juanita.

B Write the Spanish term for the language spoken in each country.

☒ Inglaterra Yo hablo _____ .

☒ Alemania Yo hablo _____ .

☑ Italia Yo hablo _italiano_____ .

☒ España Yo hablo _____ .

☑ Francia Yo hablo _frances_____ .

☑ Rusia Yo hablo _ruso_____ .

C **Complete the following mini-dialogs logically.**

EJEMPLO: Carlos: Buenos días, Señor Goya.
Señor Goya: Buenos días, <u>Carlos</u>.

1. Luis: Hola, Carlos.

Carlos: Hola, <u>Luis</u>.

2. Marcos: ¿Hablas alemán, Evita?

Evita: <u>Sí</u>, hablo alemán.

3. Amanda: ¿Hablas polaco, Alberto?

Alberto: <u>no</u>, no hablo polaco.

4. David: ¿Cómo te llamas?

Luz: <u>me</u> llamo Luz.

5. Miguel: ¿Cómo estás?

Sara: <u>Bien</u>, gracias.

10 correct

D

Sopa de letras. *Wordsearch.* Find and circle the following words and expressions.

1. por favor   Please
2. buenas noches   Good night
3. perdón   Excuse me
4. hasta luego   see you later
5. buena suerte   Good Luck

6. gracias   Thank you
7. lo siento   I'm sorry
8. adiós   Good-bye
9. de nada   you're welcome
10. hola   Hello, Hi

```
P U E D E N A D A T A O N E
M O O L A A T S O L F B R S
G Q R B G H P S O A I U O O
L S A F E R E H O D A E L I
O B G N A D R G H A R N A L
S I U A A V D T U A V A P O
I A C E A C O S S E O S D E
E R A D N I N R L A D U A H
N S L U H A S T A L U E G O
T T A A E G S O L N N R E O
O H T O N S E N D S A T B U
A I C S E I O L O A O E N P
G R A C I A S I E C H A R E
D A I B S H D A N F H T R D
R O G S A A C A D R O E E U
S A U N E N O O P V R S S E
```

E Give the following boy and girl Spanish names. Then write their names in the appropriate spaces below and complete their conversation.

(Boy's name) __Carlos__ : Hola. ¿Cómo te

_____ llamas _____ ?

(Girl's name) __Julia__ : Me __llamo Julia__ .

¿Y tú?

(Boy's name) __Carlos__ : Me llamo

__Carlos__ .

(Girl's name) __Julia__ : Mucho

__gusto__ .

(Boy's name) __carlos__ : __Encantado__ .

F With a classmate take turns greeting each other, asking and answering how things are going, and saying good-bye. Use friendly gestures, smiles, and waves.

G Look at the list of the editorial staff of *Aló,* a magazine from Colombia, and then answer the questions. (You will notice that many Spanish names for women end with the letter "a," and that many Spanish names for men end with the letter "o.")

1. What is the name of the manager *(gerente)* of the magazine?

    Andres Talero Gutierrez

2. What is the name of the director of the magazine?

    Pillar Castaño

3. How many women work in the editorial *(redacción)* department?

    _____

4. In what city is Luz María Doria a correspondent *(corresponsal)*?

   _____

5. Is Fernando Pardo in charge of photography?

   _____

6. Is Amanda Téllez the administrative director?

   _____

7. Is the person in charge of publicity in Bogotá a man or a woman?

   _____

8. Is the person in charge of supervising the production of the magazine a man or a woman?

   _____

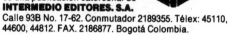

es una publicación catorcenal de
INTERMEDIO EDITORES. S.A.
Calle 93B No. 17-62. Conmutador 2189355. Télex: 45110,
44600, 44812. FAX. 2186877. Bogotá Colombia.
GERENTE
Andrés Talero Gutiérrez.
DIRECTORA
Pilar Castaño.
JEFE
Yolima Dussán.
COORDINADORA DE IMAGEN
Diana Neira.
REDACCION
Patricia Andrade Mendoza, Xiomara Martínez, Lucía Muñoz
Ortiz, María Teresa Rubino.
COLABORACION: Poncho Rentería, Lyda Citarella,
Olga Pumarejo de Sáenz, Diana Sigüenza.
CORRESPONSALES
Nacionales: Barranquilla: Rigel Castro;
Cartagena: Jacqueline Lemaitre de Basile, Edith López;
Internacionales: Miami: Luz María Doria; Nueva York:
Elizabeth Mora; París: Gilma Suárez.
DISEÑO Y DIAGRAMACION
Belisario Gómez Cardozo.
ARMADA ELECTRONICA
Carlos Antonio Medina Heredia, Pedro Nel Martínez Garavito.
FOTOGRAFIA: Fernando Pardo.
COLABORACION
Ernesto Bautista, Dora Franco, Casa Editorial EL TIEMPO.
CORRECCION
Henry Castañeda Camacho.
AGENCIAS INTERNACIONALES
Sipa-Press, N.Y. Syndication, Mondadori Press.
DIRECTORA ADMINISTRATIVA
Alexandra Téllez T.
COORDINADOR COMERCIAL
Vincenzo Moranti D.

PUBLICIDAD
Ejecutivas:
Bogotá: Yolanda García
Conmutador: 2189355–6104107.
Cali: Ingrid Pieper de González. Tel: 688781.
Medellín: Vía Comunicaciones Tel: 2816664 – 3723410.
Cartagena: Silvia de Amézquita: Tel: 645229.
Barranquilla: Marlene Cárdenas de Chegwin. Tel: 454605.
GERSAMEDIOS. Gertrudis de Saportas.
Cra. 13A No. 78-51 Of. 202 Tel: 2366568, Bogotá.
JEFE DE CIRCULACION
Nelson Cadena Cano.
SUPERVISION DE PRODUCCION
Juan Rafael Restrepo G.
FOTOMECANICA: Casa Editorial EL TIEMPO.
IMPRESION: Témpora Impresores.
DISTRIBUCION
Distribuidoras Unidas, Transversal 93 No. 52-03.
Tel: 4139666 – 4139300.
EN NUEVA YORK: Latin American. News Agency Corp. Joseph
Pezzanite. 71-22 35 th. Avenue Jackson Heights, N.Y. 11372.
Tel: (718) 478-4692. Fax (718) 458 4774.
DISTRIBUCION DE SUSCRIPCIONES
Distribuciones Lusom Ltda. Trav. 29 No. 39-47
Tel: 2448054 – 2447534.
SUSCRIPCIONES
Grupo Editorial 87 Ltda. Cra. 14 No. 79-89. Tels: 2576689 –
2181063. A.A. 55393, Bogotá.
Reclamos 2189355, Bogotá.
IMPRESO EN COLOMBIA.
PRINTED IN COLOMBIA.
Tarifa.Postal Reducida. ADPOSTAL No. 204.
PORTADA: Adriana Ricardo.
FOTO: Dora Franco.
DISEÑO DE PORTADA: ALÓ.

Unit 2

A How is each object used? Match column B with column A.

A		B
1. un libro	_____	a. lets in fresh air and daylight
2. una ventana	_____	b. gives you a place to throw used paper and trash
3. un cuadro	_____	c. makes a plain room more attractive
4. una papelera	_____	d. opens up new worlds of adventure, fantasy, travel, and information
5. un sacapuntas	_____	e. makes a dull point sharp

B Identify each of the following illustrations. (En español, por favor.)

1.  Es un _____ .

2.  Es un _____ .

3. Es una _____ .

4. Es una _____ .

5. Es un _____ .

Nombre: _____ Fecha: _____

C Name the classroom object most closely associated with the following cues. (En español, por favor.)

1. 9:00   5:30   1:45   7:52   _un reloj_
2. Guatemala   Canada   China   _un mapa_
3. *The Adventures of Huckleberry Finn*

   Moby Dick   *Sleeping Beauty*   _un libro_

D Contesta las siguientes preguntas en español. *Answer the following questions in Spanish.*

1. What can you use to make sure a line is straight?

   una regla

2. What can you use to transfer your thoughts onto paper?

   una bolígrafo

3. What can you wave at a parade?

   _____

4. What gives you a place to sit down?

   _____

5. In what can you draw pictures or keep notes?

   _____

E List six items you have in your bookbag or pencil case. (En español, por favor.)

1. _____
2. _____
3. _____
4. _____
5. _____
6. _____

F Find your way through the classroom. Name the classroom objects you encounter on your way.

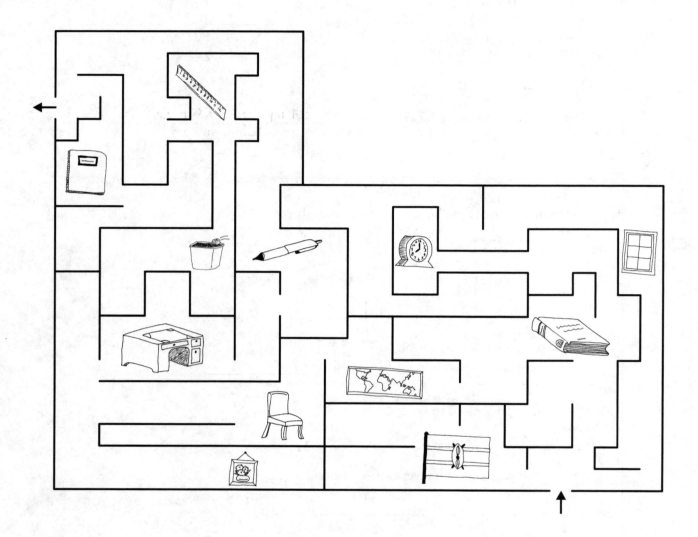

1. _____

2. _____

3. _____

4. _____

5. _____

G As you point to various classroom objects, ask a classmate for the Spanish name for each one. Keep a record of how many mistakes your classmate makes. Then reverse the roles. The winner is the person with fewer errors.

> EJEMPLO: **A:**   ¿Qué es esto?
>
> **B:**   Es un cuaderno.

H Look at the following shopping receipt for the school supplies that Patricia bought, and then answer the questions. (Patricia paid for the supplies with Colombian pesos.)

```
        *SUPERLEY*
         SUPERIOR
       MUCHAS GRACIAS
          POR SU
          VISITA
       NIT 890.900.024-B

    Fecha: 25-AGOSTO #C318034

  2 LAPICES              $100 S
  5 CUADERNOS NORMA      $750 S
  1 COLORES            $1.200 S
  1 REGLA                $250 S
  1 ESCUADRA             $300 S
  1 BOLIGRAFO AZUL        $80 S
  1 BOLIGRAFO ROJO        $80 S
  1 DICCIONARIO        $5.000 S
  1 SACAPUNTAS            $60 S
  1 LIBRO HIST         $4.100 S
  1 LIBRO MATEMAT      $5.700 S
  1 LIBRO BIOLOG       $3.500 S
  1 MAPA DEL MUNDO     $4.000 S
  1 MISCELAN           $1.000 S
  1 MISCELAN           $2.000 S
  1 MISCELAN           $1.000 S
  SUBTL              $29.120
  TOTAL              $29.120
  EFECTV             $30.000
  CAMBIO                $880

  T 14:00
```

1. Where did Patricia buy her school supplies?

   _____

2. What day did she go shopping?

   _____

3. At what time did she pay for her purchases?

   _____

4. How many pencils did she buy?

   _____

5. How much did she pay for the ruler?

   _____

6. How many pens did she buy?

   _____

7. What cost 60 pesos?

   _____

8. How many books did she buy?

   _____

9. What cost 4,000 pesos?

   _____

Unit 3

A Your friend wants you to do certain things. Circle the letter of the command he is giving you.

1. Escribe en español.

   (a.) Write in Spanish.

   b. Say it in Spanish.

2. Lee.

   a. Speak.

   (b.) Read.

3. Siéntate.

   a. Listen.

   (b.) Sit down.

4. Levanta la mano.

   (a.) Raise your hand.

   b. Go to the board.

5. Cierra el libro.

   a. Open the book.

   (b.) Close the book.

6. Saca papel.

   (a.) Take out paper.

   b. Go to the board.

B Imagine that you are Carlos' teacher and that you want him to do the following things: (1) sit down, (2) take out the book, (3) open the book, (4) read from the book, (5) close the book, and finally (6) go to the board. Number the following commands in the sequential order described.

___4___ Lee.

___1___ Siéntate.

___6___ Pasa a la pizarra.

___3___ Abre el libro.

___2___ Saca el libro.

___5___ Cierra el libro.

C Find the word in the box that best completes each command and then write it in the space provided.

español   pupltre   mano

pizarra   frases

1. Levanta la _____ .

2. Habla en _____ .

3. Pasa a la _____ .

4. Escucha las _____ .

5. Siéntate en el _____ .

D Completa las siguientes frases en forma lógica.

1. Dilo en _____ .

2. Pasa a la _____ .

3. Saca _____ .

4. Abre _____ libro.

5. Contesta la _____ .

E Write a command suggested by the word cue at the left.

1. lápiz   _____

2. libro   _____

3. música   _____

4. silla   _____

5. ventana   _____

6. mano   _____

F Working in pairs, take turns giving commands to each other. Use all the commands presented in Unit 3.

G Look at the following advertisements *(avisos)*. All of them are telling you to do something. Write the letter of each advertisement next to the appropriate English equivalent. (One of the advertisements contains a plural, informal command form; the others contain singular, formal command forms.)

a

b

c

d

e

Abra una Cuenta Corriente en Bancoop
ABRA LAS PUERTAS A TODOS SUS SERVICIOS
BANCOOP
BANCO COOPERATIVO DE COLOMBIA
El Banco de Nuestra Gente

f

ESCUCHE
A PARTIR DEL PROXIMO
LUNES 2 DE AGOSTO

LINEA UNIVERSITARIA
bajo la conducción de
LUZ ELENA CASTILLO y
JOSE MARIA PULIDO
de Lunes a Viernes de 7 a 9 de la mañana
además
EDICION DEL MEDIO DIA
con Surya Inés y José Díaz Betancourt
a las 2 de la tarde
CIERRE INFORMATIVO
con Alberto Osorio y Karla Planter
a las 7 de la noche

4.3 Mhz
FM
STEREO
RADIO UNIVERSIDAD

g

RECORTE ESTE AVISO Y
GANESE US$300

_____*k*_____ 1. Reserve a room at the Inter-Continental Hotel.

_____*g*_____ 2. Win 300 dollars.

_____*e*_____ 3. Open the doors to all your services.

_____*d*_____ 4. Call us.

_____*f*_____ 5. Listen to the university radio.

_____*c*_____ 6. Do not ignore the risks.

_____*b*_____ 7. Study color television electronics today.

H Crucigrama. Complete the following crossword puzzle with vocabulary from this unit.

Vertical

1. "...las frases."
2. commands
4. Be seated.
6. Read.
9. "...el libro."
10. "Contesta la...."
11. "...en español."
13. "...a la pizarra."

Horizontal

1. Answer.
3. words
4. "A palabras necias, oídos...."
5. Repeat.
7. Open.
8. Listen.
12. Write.
14. "...papel."
15. Speak.

Unit 4

A Circle the letter that tells how many items are in each group.

1.   a. dieciséis   (b.) diez   c. nueve

2. 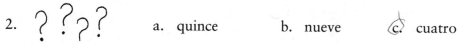   a. quince   b. nueve   (c.) cuatro

3.   (a.) siete   b. seis   c. ocho

4.   (a.) uno   b. once   c. diez

5.   a. treinta   b. trece   (c.) tres

B Match the words in column B with the Arabic numerals in column A.

A		B
1. 2	d	a. trece
2. 8	e	b. cinco
3. 13	a	c. veintiuno
4. 5	b	d. dos
5. 21	c	e. ocho

C Nursery rhymes and classic children's tales. Circle the letter of the correct answer.

1. How many lambs did Mary have?

   a. uno   (b.) once

2. How many little pigs were there?

   a. seis   (b.) tres

3. How many dwarfs did Snow White meet?

   (a.) siete   b. nueve

4. How many stepsisters did Cinderella have?

   (a.) dos   b. doce

5. How many blackbirds were baked in the pie?

   (a.) veintitrés   b. veinticuatro

D Find the pattern and then write the missing numbers in Spanish.

1. cuarenta, _curente_ , sesenta

2. dieciocho, _diecihueve_ , veinte

3. seis, _siete_ , ocho

4. cinco, _dies_ , quince

5. setenta, _ochenta_ , noventa

Nombre: _____ Fecha: _____

 E Contesta las siguientes preguntas en español.

1. How many planets are there in our solar system?

   nueve

2. How many toes does a person have?

   dies

3. How many feet does a duck have?

   dos

4. How many weeks make up a year?

   cuatro

5. How many letters are there in the English alphabet?

   venti sies

6. How many days are there in the month of November?

   trenta

7. How many items make up a dozen?

   dose

8. How many minutes make up three-quarters of an hour?

   cuarenta cinco

 F Solve the following math problems in Spanish.

1. Tres por cuatro son _dose_ .

2. Siete y quince son _rente uho_ .

3. Mil menos quinientos son _____ .

4. Dieciséis dividido por ocho son _____ .

5. Trienta y cuarenta y uno son _____ .

6. Noventa por cinco son _____ .

7. Veintiocho dividido por cuatro son _____ .

8. Doscientos menos ciento y uno son _____ .

G With a partner see how good you are with numbers. Each of you receives 25 points at the beginning. Whenever either one of you makes a mistake counting, subtract one point. To begin, you start counting at one and then suddenly stop. Your partner should continue counting and then stop at any time. You should be quick enough to pick up the numbers. Continue counting and alternating until you reach 50 or another previously designated number. The player with more points at the end wins.

H Imagine that you are shopping for holiday gifts. Because you are careful with the money you spend, you always check prices. Look at the catalog page from Hogarama, a department store in Guatemala, and then answer in Spanish the questions below. (The monetary unit of Guatemala is the quetzal; the plural is quetzales. The quetzal is represented by the letter "Q.")

1. ¿Qué *(What)* cuesta ciento cincuenta y cuatro quetzales con *(with)* noventa y cinco centavos *(cents)?*

   _____

2. ¿Cuánto cuesta la vajilla de porcelana fina de cuarenta y cinco piezas?

   _____

   _____

3. ¿Cuánto cuesta el tostador?

   _____

4. ¿Cuántos vasos de diecisiete onzas hay?

   _____

5. ¿Cuántas piezas de cristal hay en la vajilla de cocina Visions?

   _____

6. ¿Cuánto cuesta el exprimidor de cítricos con base de cristal?

   _____

7. ¿Cuánto cuesta el pichel de vidrio?

   _____

8. ¿Cuestan las ollas Rochedo más o menos de *(more or less than)* cien quetzales?

   _____

Nombre: _____ Fecha: _____

Q166.⁹⁸

Set de ollas ROCHEDO
américano de teflón 7 piezas:

SUMBEAM BATIDORA
MIXMAXTER
MIXER
6 VELOCIDADES

ESPECIAL Q.278.95
MENSUAL Q.60.00

PERCOLADORA DRIP
ESPECIAL Q.154.95

**OLLAS PRESION
ROCHEDO - 6 Y 8 LITROS
DESDE Q.188.95**

**EXPRIMIDOR CITRICOS
OSTER
ESPECIAL Q.160.95**

Pichel de vidrio de
80 onzas, LIBBEY:

Q17.⁹⁸

Vajilla de porcelana fina
CORELLE, 45 piezas.:

Q455.⁹⁸

Exprimidor de cítricos, con base
de cristal.:

Q12.⁹⁸

Q13.⁹⁸

6 vasos de 17 onzas LIBBEY:

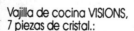

**TOSTADOR PROCTOR SILEX
2 RODAJAS
ESPECIAL Q.92.95**

Vajilla de cocina VISIONS,
7 piezas de cristal.:

Q202.⁹⁸

Hogarama
Su hogar es algo muy nuestro

Ofertas válidas hasta el 15 de agosto o hasta agotar existencias. Compare nuestros precios. Consulte
nuestros planes de financiamiento.
Todas nuestras tiendas abiertas domingos

Exploring Spanish

19

Unit 5

 A For what is each of the following cities famous? Match column B with column A.

A			B	
1.	Saltillo	_____	a.	university center of Mexico
2.	Mérida	_____	b.	capital city of Spain
3.	Madrid	*b*	c.	city of Mayan architecture
4.	Sevilla	*c*	d.	capital city of Andalucía
5.	Málaga	*d*	e.	city of Moorish heritage

B After studying the maps of Spain and Mexico and reading the information about these countries in your textbook, circle the letter of the correct answer to each of the following questions.

1. Which river flows westward into the Atlantic?

   a. Río Duero   b. Río Ebro   c. Río Bravo

2. What is the name of the sea north of Spain?

   a. Golfo de México   b. Mar Mediterráneo   c. Mar Cantábrico

3. What is Spain's largest inland port?

   a. Sevilla   b. Madrid   c. Málaga

4. What is the name of Mexico's dual mountain chain?

   a. Los Pirineos   b. Sierra Madre   c. Sierra Nevada

5. What did the Aztec and Mayan Indians build?

   a. transoceanic highways   b. advanced civilizations   c. shopping centers

C Looking at the maps of Spain and Mexico in your textbook, identify the direction you travel from one city to another. Use the following codes: N (north), NE (northeast), S (south), SE (southeast), E (east), NW (northwest), W (west), SW (southwest).

FROM	TO	DIRECTION
1. Mérida	Acapulco	_____
2. Veracruz	Saltillo	_____
3. México D.F.	Acapulco	_____
3. Granada	Sevilla	NW
4. Madrid	Barcelona	NE
5. Málaga	Madrid	S

D Contesta las siguientes preguntas sobre los ríos en español.

1. What river flows west from La Mancha to the border of Portugal?

   Tajo

2. What do Mexicans call the "Río Grande"?

   _____

3. What city does the Guadalquivir River flow through?

   Sevilla

4. What is the longest river in Spain?

   Tajo

5. Are all the rivers in Spain navigable?

   NO

6. What sea does the Ebro River empty into?

   Mediterranean

7. Does the Duero River flow into the Atlantic Ocean?

   _____

E Look at the maps of Spain and Mexico. Find the following cities and rivers and then write their names in the appropriate spaces.

Acapulco	Barcelona	Río Grande	Málaga
Granada	México D.F.	Río Tajo	Saltillo
Mérida	Río Guadiana	Veracruz	Madrid

1. _____   7. _____

2. _____   8. _____

3. _____   9. _____

4. _____   10. _____

5. _____   11. _____

6. _____   12. _____

Nombre: _____ Fecha: _____

 F Crucigrama. Complete the following crossword puzzle with information from this unit.

Vertical

2. The Tajo River empties into this ocean.
3. river that drains north central and northwestern Spain
5. sea north of Spain
6. city located on the Guadalquivir River
7. sea

Horizontal

1. Spain's capital
4. center of tourism and a popular beach resort in Mexico
8. This is the only Spanish-speaking country in North America.
9. "Sierra..."
10. city that lies southwest of Mexico D.F. and is a site of Mayan culture
11. river that flows through Toledo
12. only river in Spain that flows eastward

G Imagine that you are inquiring about a trip to Spain at a travel agency. Ask your partner, a travel agent, about what you can see and do there and what you should pack for a two-week stay. Decide on a particular month so that you can plan appropriate clothing. Then reverse the roles so that your classmate can play the role of the traveler, this time inquiring about a trip to Mexico.

H Take a look at the map of the routes of Avianca Airlines and then fill in the blanks with the appropriate information.

1. Avianca is an airline from _____ .

2. The only Mexican city that Avianca flies to is
    _____ City.

3. The southern city in South America that Avianca flies to is
    _____ , the capital of Argentina.

4. Uruguay, Paraguay, and _____ are the only three
    Spanish-speaking countries in South America that Avianca does not fly to.

5. _____ is the only city in the Caribbean that Avianca
    flies to.

6. The only Central American country that Avianca flies to is
    _____ .

7. Venezuela, Ecuador, Peru, and Chile are four _____
    American countries that Avianca flies to.

8. Cuba and _____ are two Spanish-speaking islands
    that Avianca does not fly to.

9. Guatemala, El Salvador, _____ , Nicaragua, and Costa
    Rica are five Spanish speaking countries in Central America that Avianca does not fly to.

10. If you are traveling to Europe with Avianca, your plane will stop in
    _____ , the capital of Venezuela.

Nombre: ______________________ Fecha: ______________

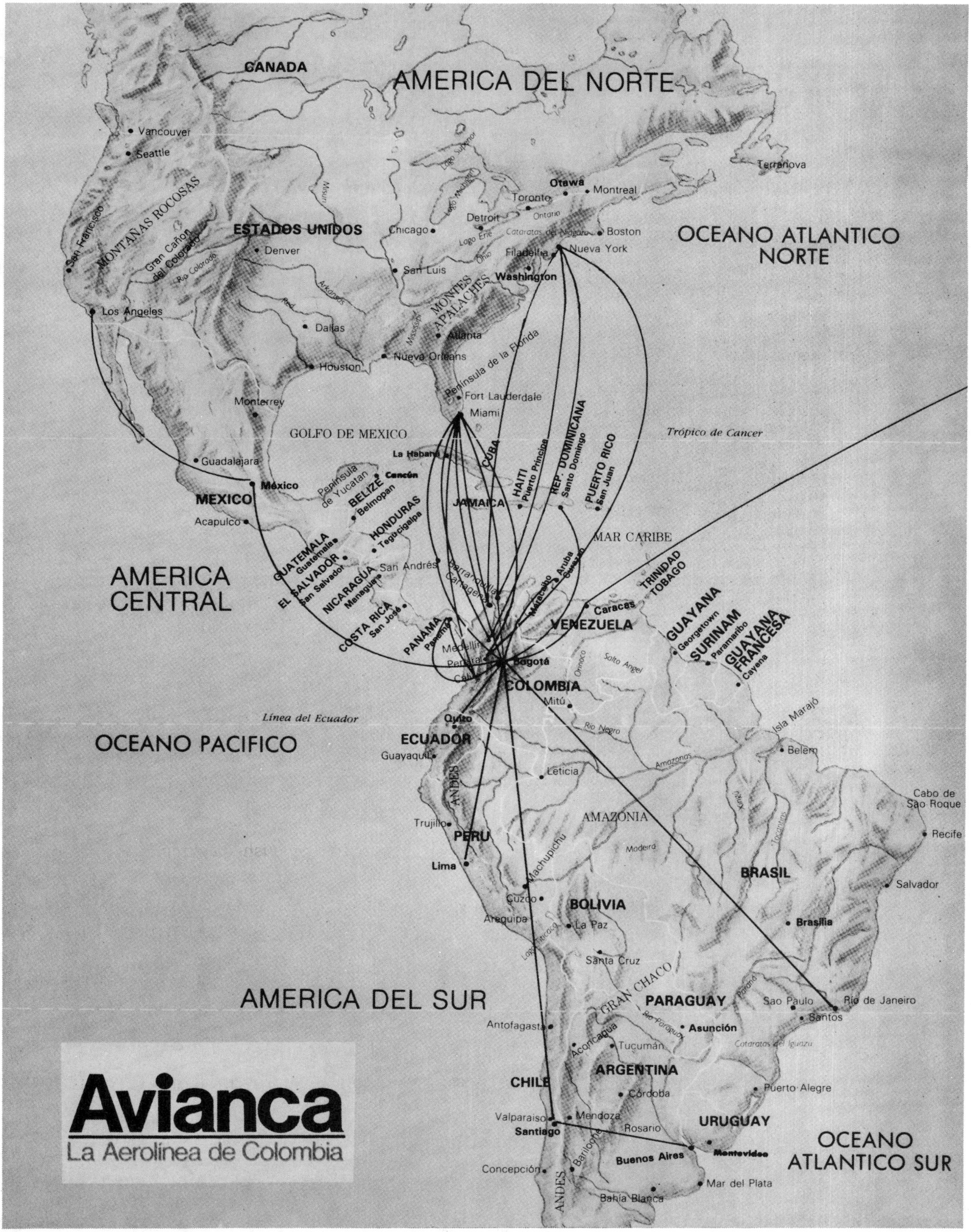

Nombre: _____ Fecha: _____ Unit ___

Unit 6

A Where do you usually do the following things? Match column B with column A.

      A   B

1. cook   _____   a. en el jardín
2. sleep   _____   b. en la sala
3. take a shower   _____   c. en la cocina
4. eat   _____   d. en la alcoba
5. park the car   _____   e. en el baño
6. plant flowers   _____   f. en el comedor
7. receive visitors   _____   g. en el garaje

B What could you find in each of the following rooms? Circle the appropriate item.

sala:	dishwasher	recliner	bathtub	microwave
baño:	sofa	blender	silverware	shower
cocina:	refrigerator	bed	car	computer
alcoba:	lawn mower	kitchen table	bed	sink
garaje:	plates	automotive tools	pillowcases	stove
comedor:	broom	clothes closet	snow shovel	tablecloth

C Write in Spanish the appropriate questions for the following answers.

1. ¿ _____ ?

   Vivo en un apartamento en Houston.

2. ¿ _____ ?

   Hay dos baños en mi casa.

3. ¿ _____ ?

   La cocina está detrás del comedor.

4. ¿ _____ ?

   Hay tres alcobas en mi casa.

D Completa el siguiente diálogo en español. (Make up any information you wish.)

Susana: ¿Dónde vives?

Tú: Vivo en _____ .

Susana: ¿Está el garaje detrás del jardín?

Tú: _____ está.

Susana: ¿Cuántas alcobas hay en tu casa?

Tú: Hay _____ .

Susana: ¿Cuántos baños hay en tu casa?

Tú: Hay _____ .

Susana: ¿Hay un patio en tu casa?

Tú: _____ un patio en mi casa.

Susana: ¿Cuántas ventanas hay en la sala de tu casa?

Tú: Hay _____ .

E   Draw a floor plan of your house and then label the rooms in Spanish.

F Find your way back to your bed. Name each type of house or shelter you encounter on your way.

1. _____
2. _____
3. _____
4. _____
5. _____

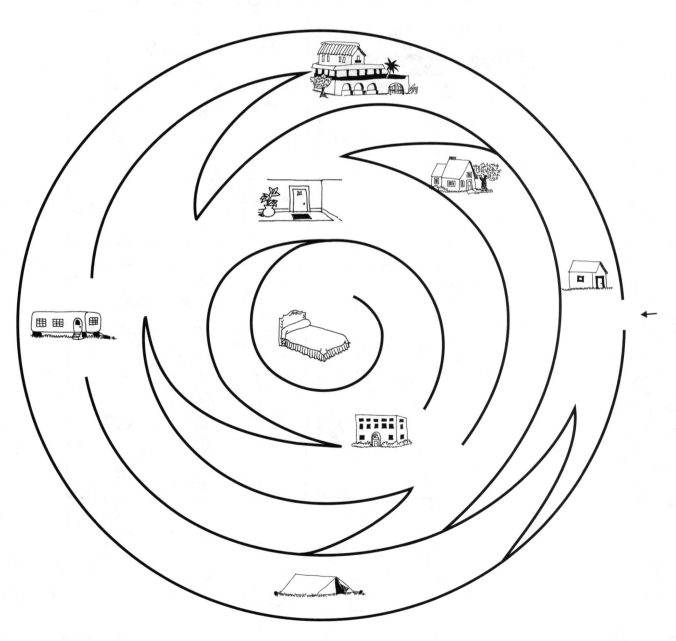

G Imagine that you are a real estate agent. Based on the advertisements, advise the people that follow where to buy a house or an apartment according to what they want.

EJEMPLO: Sr. Vargas: Quiero *(I want)* una casa de ciento noventa y cuatro metros cuadrados.

Tú: Compre en *(Buy in)* Casas Valle del Lili.

RINCON del campestre
C O N D O M I N I O
TORRE DOS

Con la mejor vista sobre los campos de golf del Club Campestre, entrando por la Calle 5a.

- Apartamentos exclusivos de 336 m²
- 3 parqueaderos por apartamento
- 2 ascensores (1 semipanorámico), sistema de gas, planta eléctrica de emergencia, compactador de basuras, cofre de seguridad.
- Piscina, 2 antenas parabólicas, circuito cerrado de T.V., baño turco y sauna.
- Apatamentos con ascensor privado, Hall de acceso, 3 alcobas cada una con baño y vestier, Hall de alcobas, biblioteca, terraza, cocina integral, sala, comedor, comedor auxiliar, zona de oficios, alcoba doble de servicios con baño.

conjunto residencial
Bagatelle

En la nueva Urbanización El Polo Club en Ciudad Jardín, apartamentos desde 189 hasta 265 Mts₂

- 27,000 Mts. de exclusivas zonas verdes
- Ciclovías y Circuito Personal
- Tres (3) piscinas
- Ductos para aire acondicionado
- Salón Social • Teléfono y Depósito
- Sauna, Turco, Solarium
- Planta Eléctrica
- Ascensores • Parqueadero Visitantes
- 3 Parqueaderos por Apto.
- Apartamentos con 3 Alcobas
- Terraza y Balcones
- Estar - T.V. o Biblioteca

nuevas
CASAS DE EL CANEY

"Nuevas" casas de El Caney:

- "110 M² • Sala - comedor • Cocina • Dos jardines interiores • Baño social completo • Zona de oficios • Alcoba de servicio con baño • Alcoba principal con baño • Alcoba principal con baño y vestier • Dos alcobas • Baño auxiliar • Estadero de T.V. o cuarta alcoba • Garaje cubierto • Teléfono • Y ahora entrando por la carrera 86".

CASAS
VALLE DEL LILI

Casas de dos pisos entre 145 y 194 metros cuadrados.

Con garaje cubierto, depósito, sala, comedor, baño social, terraza cubierta, jardín interior, cocina integral, alcoba de servicio con baño y patio de ropas.

Dos alcobas una con vestier y baño de alcobas, alcoba principal con dos closets, baño y balcón.

Las casas más grandes tienen garaje doble, jardín exterior, estar de T.V. con terraza, closet de linos y una de las alcobas con baño.

1. Sra. Calderón: Quiero vivir *(to live)* en un edificio de apartamentos con tres piscinas.

    Tú: _____

    _____ .

2. Srta. Salgado: Quiero una casa con dos jardines interiores.

    Tú: _____

    _____ .

3. Sr. Padilla: Quiero un apartamento de trescientos treinta y seis metros cuadrados.

    Tú: _____

    _____ .

4. Srta. Ordóñez: Quiero una casa con garaje cubierto y depósito.

    Tú: _____

    _____ .

5. Sr. González: Quiero vivir en un apartamento con ascensor privado.

    Tú: _____

    _____ .

6. Sra. Rangel: Quiero una casa de ciento diez metros cuadrados.

    Tú: _____

    _____ .

7. Sr. Méndez: Quiero vivir en un edificio de apartamentos con aire acondicionado.

    Tú: _____

    _____ .

Draw a floor plan of your dream house. Then, working in pairs, give your partner a tour of the house, pointing out different rooms and other features and saying *"Aquí está... (Here is...)"*. Your partner will ask you for the location of several rooms that you have not mentioned, and you will answer, saying *"Aquí está (Here it is)"* or *"Está detrás del...."* When you have finished, switch roles and do the activity again. Here are some expressions you may want to know:

la casa de mis sueños = my dream house	**el sótano** = basement
el lavadero = laundry room	**la biblioteca** = library
la sala de televisión = T.V. room	**la terraza** = terrace
el gimnasio = gym	**la piscina** = swimming pool
el pasillo = hallway	**la escalera** = stairs
la planta baja = main floor	**el primer piso** = second floor
la sauna = sauna	**el jacuzzi** = jacuzzi

EJEMPLO: **A:** Aquí está la casa de mis sueños. En la casa hay muchos cuartos. Hay cinco alcobas y cinco baños. Aquí está la sala y aquí está el comedor. Aquí en el jardín está la piscina y detrás está el gimnasio.

B: ¿Dónde está tu alcoba?

A: Aquí está.

B: ¿Y dónde está el garaje?

A: Está detrás de la casa.

Unit 7

A Match column B with column A.

A		B
1. godparents _____		a. chico
2. girl _____		b. nieto
3. baby _____		c. tío
4. boy _____		d. nene
5. niece _____		e. prima
6. aunt _____		f. sobrino
7. grandson _____		g. tía
8. nephew _____		h. sobrina
9. cousin _____		i. muchacha
10. uncle _____		j. padrinos

B Completa las siguientes frases.

1. El hijo de mi hermano es mi _____ .

2. La hermana de mi madre es mi _____ .

3. Los hijos de mis padres son mis _____ .

4. Mi hermana es la _____ de mis abuelos.

5. El hijo de mi tío es mi _____ .

6. Mi madre es la _____ de mi padre.

7. Mi padre y mi madre son mis _____ .

8. Mis abuelos, mis tíos, y mis primos son mis _____ .

In the spaces provided write the names of the members of your favorite television family. Only use those spaces that apply.

1. padre   _____

2. madre   _____

3. hermano(s)   _____

    _____

    _____

4. hermana(s)   _____

    _____

    _____

5. tío(s)   _____

    _____

    _____

6. tía(s)   _____

    _____

    _____

7. abuelo(s)   _____

    _____

    _____

8. abuela(s)   _____

    _____

    _____

D Make your own family tree by labeling each person's name and his or her relationship to you. Start at the bottom by labeling yourself and any brothers or sisters you may have. Next, show your parents, your aunts and uncles, your cousins, your grandparents, etc. Some new words that you might need are:

padrastro = stepfather   **madrastra** = stepmother

hermanastro = stepbrother   **hermanastra** = stepsister

E ¿Cuántos? Contesta las siguientes preguntas en español.

EJEMPLOS: ¿Cuántos sobrinos tienes *(do you have)*?
No tengo *(I don't have any)* sobrinos./Tengo *(I have)* un sobrino.

¿Cuántas sobrinas tienes?
No tengo sobrinas./Tengo una sobrina.

1. ¿Cuántos hermanos tienes?

_____

2. ¿Cuántas hermanas tienes?

_____

3. ¿Cuántas primas tienes?

_____

4. ¿Cuántos primos tienes?

_____

5. ¿Cuántas tías tienes?

_____

6. ¿Cuántos tíos tienes?

_____

7. ¿Cuántas sobrinas tienes?

_____

8. ¿Cuántos sobrinos tienes?

_____

F Crucigrama. Complete the following crossword puzzle with vocabulary from this unit.

Vertical

1. mother
2. aunt
3. husband and wife
4. sister
5. godfather
9. grandmother
10. grandfather
11. grandson
13. sons and daughters
15. niece
17. granddaughter

Horizontal

5. relatives
6. parents
7. wife
8. godmother
12. another word for "chico"
14. another word for "criatura"
16. aunts and uncles
18. nephew
19. another word for "muchacha"
20. father
21. cousins (f.)

G Bring pictures of various members of your family to class. Working in pairs, your partner should point to certain people in your photos and ask who they are and what their names are. You should respond appropriately. When you have finished, switch roles.

EJEMPLO: A: ¿Quién es?
            B: Es mi madrina.
            A: ¿Cómo se llama?
            B: Se llama María.

H Look at the announcements for different family occasions published in a newspaper in Latin America. Then read the statements that follow, decide whether they are true (*verdad*) or false (*falso*), and write V or F in the spaces provided. Some expressions that you may need to know are:

contraerán matrimonio = will get married
fueron = were
nombres = names
nueva jurista = new lawyer
pequeña = little

Enma Ivonne Labbé Turcios se graduó

La recipiendaria es hija de los estimados esposos, licenciado Olegario Labbé Morales y de la señora Martha Turcios de Labbé. Fueron padrinos de la nueva jurista la licenciada Carmen Ellgutter Figueroa y los abogados Boanerges Amílcar Mejía Orellana, Carlos Estuardo Gálvez Barrios y su padre Olegario Antonio Labbé Morales.

El acontecimiento fue festejado con una reunión de familiares y amigos quienes le desearon a la nueva profesional de la ley éxitos en la carrera que inicia. Enviamos un saludo a Enma Ivonne y le deseamos éxitos en el foro guatemalteco.

ANNY BEATRIZ LUQUE SANTO-YO y el teniente de infantería de marina Pablo Roberto Enciso Pinilla, hijos de Alfredo Luque Saavedra y Beatriz Santoyo de Luque, y de Roberto Enciso Beltrán y Sara Pinilla de Enciso, contraerán matrimonio el domingo próximo a la una de la tarde en la iglesia de Santa Bibiana. Luego, los padres de la novia ofrecerán una recepción en el Museo del Chicó.

ANIVERSARIO
Hernando Atehortúa Ch. y Lucy Sierra F.

Hoy, 4 de agosto, cumplen 30 años de vida matrimonial los esposos Hernando Atehortúa Chalarca y señora Lucy Sierra Flórez. Son sus hijos: Carlos Mario, casado con Sandra Jiménez Londoño; Hernando David, casado con Zoraida Guerra Diosa; Hamilton Alveiro, casado con Ivon Yanet Cifuentes Yepez; Oswaldo; Marcela y Walter Mauricio. Cuentan además con sus nietos Diego Alejandro, Sergio David y Yeyson Alejandro.

Por tal motivo han dispuesto la celebración de una Misa en acción de gracias, en la Parroquia San Francisco de Asís, el próximo 8 de agosto, con asistencia de familiares y amigos.

BAUTIZO

Con los nombres de María Paula fue bautizada la niña llegada al hogar de Guillermo Rubiano Carreño y señora Olga Mercedes Delgado de Rubiano. La pequeña es nieta de Gustavo Rubiano y señora Inés Carreño de Rubiano

Ha fallecido cristianamente el señor
Joel David Cartaya Pérez
(Q.E.P.D.)

Su esposa, Julia Pérez de Cartaya; sus hijos, David Manuel, Yuly e Irma Cartaya Pérez; su hijo político, Germán José González; sus nietos: Daminger, Marian y Naomi; su hermana, Irma de Alas; sobrinos, primos, demás familiares y amigos, invitan a sus amistades al acto del sepelio que se efectuará hoy, a las 9:00 am, en El Cementerio General del Sur.
Dirección: Funeraria Los Caobos, Capilla Nº 1, avenida Libertador, Los Caobos.

1. _____ Lucy Sierra Flórez and her husband are celebrating their 30th wedding anniversary.

2. _____ David Manuel, Yuly, and Irma Cartaya Pérez are cousins of Joel David Cartaya Pérez.

3. _____ Little María Paula is Gustavo Rubiano's granddaughter.

4. _____ The godparents of the new lawyer were Olegario Labbé Morales and Martha Turcios de Labbé.

5. _____ Anny Beatriz Luque Santoyo is the daughter of Alfredo and Beatriz.

6. _____ The name of the child that was baptized is María Paula.

7. _____ Diego Alejandro, Sergio David, and Yeyson Alejandro are sons of Hernando Atehortúa Chalarca and Lucy Sierra Flórez.

8. _____ The parents of Enma Ivonne Turcios are Olegario and Martha.

9. _____ Anny Beatriz Luque Santoyo will be Pablo Roberto Enciso Pinilla's wife.

10. _____ Irma de Alas is Joel David's brother.

Unit 8

 A Match the skills in column B with the jobs in column A.

A		B
1. mecánico _____		a. has good sense of rhythm
2. cocinero _____		b. knows how and when to plant crops
3. electricista _____		c. can help you with your health
4. carpintero _____		d. has good sense of color and perspective
5. médico _____		e. knows how to fix an engine
6. actor _____		f. can create appetizing delicacies
7. músico _____		g. imitates well and memorizes early
8. plomero _____		h. knows hard wood from soft wood
9. granjero _____		i. knows how to bring electricity into a house
10. artista _____		j. can repair a leaking faucet

B Circle the letter of the subject area most closely associated with each occupation.

1. médico

   a. anatomy   b. music   c. botany

2. músico

   a. geography   b. fashion   c. band

3. granjero

   a. art   b. agriculture   c. literature

4. comerciante

   a. drama   b. engineering   c. marketing

5. cocinero

   a. nutrition   b. history   c. math

6. actor

   a. chemistry   b. physics   c. drama

C Name the person you would call in each of the following circumstances.

EJEMPLOS: Your car will not start.
Necesito llamar a *(I need to call)* un <u>mecánico</u>.

The bathroom sink is clogged.
Necesito llamar a una <u>plomera</u>.

1. You need someone to build cabinets for your kitchen.

Necesito llamar a una _____ .

2. You've sprained your ankle.

Necesito llamar a un _____ .

3. You are making a movie and need a woman to play a principal character.

Necesito llamar a una _____ .

4. You've invented a new product. You want someone to sell it for you.

Necesito llamar a una _____ .

5. Your grandfather is ill. You need to find someone to take care of him during the day.

Necesito llamar a un _____ .

D Completa el siguiente diálogo en forma lógica. Usa *(Use)* las palabras del recuadro *(box)*.

> cartero   cocinera   empleo   profesora
>
> dedicas   enfermero   qué   profesión   Cuál

Sara: ¿A qué te _____ ?

Luis: Soy _____ . Y tú,

        ¿a _____ te dedicas?

Sara: Soy _____ de español.

        ¿ _____ es la profesión de tu hermano?

Luis: Es _____ en un hospital. ¿Cuál es la

        _____ de tu prima?

Sara: Es _____ en un hotel de Madrid.

Luis: ¡Oh!, mi padrino también tiene *(also has)* un _____

        en Madrid.

E Working in pairs, you and your partner should each make a list of five cues. Each cue should correspond to one of the occupations you have learned in this unit. Then take turns telling one another the cues and guessing the occupations they are associated with. If you or your partner cannot correctly identify an occupation on the first try, keep guessing.

EJEMPLOS: **A:**   "Orchestra."

                B: *Músico.*

                A: *¡Sí!*

                B: "Tractor."

                A: *Carpintero./Carpintera.*

                B: *No.*

                A: *Agricultor./Agricultora.*

                B: *¡Sí!*

F Contesta las siguientes preguntas en español.

1. Who generally works in a field?

   _____

2. Who generally works on a stage?

   _____

3. Who generally works with a doctor?

   _____

4. Who generally works in a classroom?

   _____

5. Who generally works in a kitchen?

   _____

6. Who generally works with a band?

   _____

7. Who generally works in a garage?

   _____

8. Who generally works in a post office?

   _____

G *Buscando trabajo.* Imagine that you are looking for a job in Venezuela. Refer to the classified section of *El Universal,* a Venezuelan newspaper, and decide which advertisements correspond with what you want to do.

a

POLICLINICA METROPOLITANA
Solicita

Enfermeras

— Experiencia reconocida en Areas de:
Quirófano, Terapia Intensiva y Hospitalización
— Buena presencia
— Capacidad de relacionarse
— Disponibilidad inmediata

La empresa ofrece:

— Agradable ambiente de trabajo
— Remuneración acorde con la experiencia
— Posibilidad de ascenso
— Curso de actualización
— Póliza de HCM y accidentes personales
— Planes de ahorros
— Becas de estudios
— Otros beneficios socio-económicos

b

SE SOLICITA

RECEPCIONISTA

— Buena presencia
— Preferiblemente viva en zona adyacente a La Trinidad
— Excelente habilidad para trato con el público

Concertar cita por los teléfonos:
941.7745 - 93.35.57 - 93.25.57.

c

PARATE
Encontraste Empleo
Importante Compañía Multinacional Solicita:

10 Profesionales (diferentes áreas)
8 Estudiantes, cualquier área (nocturno)
4 Secretarias
5 Auxiliares Contables
6 Modelos
5 Técnicos (diversas áreas)

d

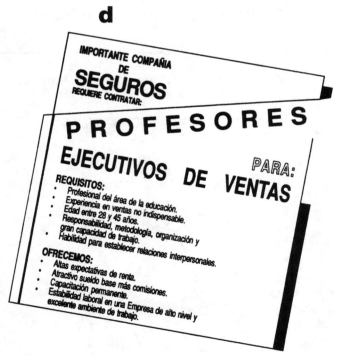

IMPORTANTE COMPAÑIA DE
SEGUROS
REQUIERE CONTRATAR:

PROFESORES
EJECUTIVOS DE VENTAS
PARA:

REQUISITOS:
• Profesional del área de la educación.
• Experiencia en ventas no indispensable.
• Edad entre 28 y 45 años.
• Responsabilidad, metodología, organización y gran capacidad de trabajo.
• Habilidad para establecer relaciones interpersonales.

OFRECEMOS:
• Altas expectativas de renta.
• Atractivo sueldo base más comisiones.
• Capacitación permanente.
• Estabilidad laboral en una Empresa de alto nivel y excelente ambiente de trabajo.

e

SE SOLICITA
SECRETARIA EJECUTIVA
CON AMPLIOS CONOCIMIENTOS
ADMINISTRATIVOS, VENTAS,
MANEJO DE MICROS:
(LOTUS - WINDOWS - WORD STAR)
INFORMACION POR LOS TELFS: 862.66.51 - 83.56.53 - 83.58.60

f

EMPRESA TEXTIL
SOLICITA

MENSAJERO

– Joven de 18 a 25 años
– Mínimo 3er. año de bachillerato
– Experiencia en trámites bancarios

Interesados presentarse con documentos y foto reciente a:
Esquina de Romualda con avenida Fuerzas Armadas, Edf. Ver-
dmont, mezzanina 1.
En horario de 8:30 am a 11:30 am y de 2:30 pm a 4:30 pm.

g

PILOTO ●

Se solicita para Merlin III-C

Interesados presentar currícu-
lum vitae en el Centro Banaven,
entrada "D", piso 2, Ofic. D-22,
Avenida La Estancia, Chuao.

h

Se Solicita

Ingeniero Electricista o Mecánico

Experiencia de 3 a 5 años. Area comercial, motores y
generadores eléctricos y servicios a los mismos para
actuar en el mercado venezolano.
Solicitar entrevista: 283.4463, Caracas.

1. _____ I'd like to work as a messenger.

2. _____ I'd like to find a job as a receptionist.

3. _____ I'm looking for a plane to fly.

4. _____ I'd like to help people who are ill.

5. _____ I'd like to teach people how to sell things.

6. _____ I'm looking for an electrical engineering job.

7. _____ I want to work as a model.

8. _____ I'm looking for a secretarial position.

Crucigrama. Complete the following crossword puzzle with information from this unit.

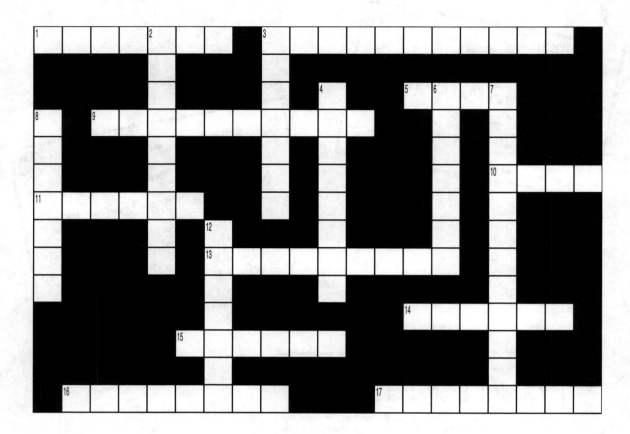

Vertical

2. "El...hace maestro."
3. distributes packages and letters
4. milks cows and plants seeds (m.)
6. paints, draws, etches and illustrates
7. installs electrical power
8. repairs faucets and pipes (m.)
12. "¿A qué te...?"

Horizontal

1. "Agencia de..."
3. runs a business
5. "El ejercicio...maestro."
9. saws wood (f.)
10. "¿...es tu profesión?"
11. interprets musical masterpieces
13. tends to sick people (f.)
14. diagnoses an illness (f.)
15. performs a theatrical role (f.)
16. teaches a class
17. we're looking for

Unit 9

A Circle the letter of the item that corresponds with each of the following situations.

1. You are thirsty.

   a. galleta   b. queso   c. huevo   d. jugo

2. You are hungry.

   a. agua mineral   b. sal   c. bistec   d. servilleta

3. You want to eat fruit.

   a. pollo   b. pera   c. pudín   d. pan

4. You are going to have some soup and need a utensil.

   a. cuchara   b. florero   c. mantequilla   d. servilleta

5. You want some dessert.

   a. espinaca   b. salchicha   c. helado   d. sangría

B You are having guests for a special dinner this evening. Create a menu. (En español, por favor.)

Appetizer: _____ and crackers

Main Dish (specialty): _____

Vegetables: _____ and

_____

Dessert: _____

Beverages: _____ and

_____

C Match the Spanish expression in column B with its corresponding description in column A.

A		B
1. The seasoning some people put on french fries.	_____	a. azúcar
2. What you spread on bread.	_____	b. taza
3. What you drink milk from.	_____	c. vaso
4. What you add to sweeten something.	_____	d. mantel
5. What you cut meat with.	_____	e. cuchara
6. What you drink coffee from.	_____	f. sal
7. The first meal of the day.	_____	g. desayuno
8. What you eat soup with.	_____	h. cuchillo
9. What covers the table.	_____	i. mantequilla

D Circle the letter of the correct answer to each question.

1. Which famous dish comes from Cuba?

   a. arroz con pollo   b. ropa vieja   c. fresas con nata

2. Which specialty comes from the province of Valencia?

   a. tacos   b. paella   c. flan caramelo

3. Where did thick hot chocolate originate?

   a. México   b. España   c. Argentina

4. What is made of ground beef, tomatoes, onion, green peppers and beans?

   a. churros   b. tortilla española   c. chile con carne

5. Which dish comes in folded tortillas?

   a. tacos   b. fresas con nata   c. churros

6. Which dessert is made with strawberries?

   a. flan caramelo   b. churros   c. fresas con nata

E Descifra las palabras.

1. LOPOL _____

2. LEGALAST _____

3. DEHALO _____

4. YUADESON _____

5. REVILTASLE _____

6. TELNAQIMLAU _____

7. REBAMH _____

8. EUHSOV _____

9. SHACCHASIL _____

10. DES _____

F With your partner draw pictures of the foods, beverages and tableware whose Spanish names you have learned. Instead of drawing you may choose to find pictures of these items in back issues of magazines or newspapers. Then cut out these pictures. Take turns with your partner showing a picture as your partner identifies it. Alternate showing and naming objects until all pictures are identified. See who can name the most items correctly.

EJEMPLO: **A:** Shows a picture of a glass to **B**.

B: Says "*Es un vaso.*"

G Your friend invites you to his or her house for a snack. Ask in Spanish what there is to eat. You will get a choice of three fruits, some cookies or ice cream. Say "Good, I am hungry. Thank you." Then select one of the choices (*en español*, of course).

H Look at the following menu of a restaurant in Spain, and then answer the questions *(en español)*. Here are some expressions that you may need to know:

primer = first   **segundo** = second

plato = dish   **verdura** = vegetables

calamares = squid   **postre** = dessert

a la plancha = on the grill

Menú

PRIMER PLATO:

      PAELLA MIXTA

      HABAS A LA HUERTANA

      SOPA DE CALDO

      VERDURA

      ENSALADA VERDE

SEGUNDO PLATO:

      POLLO A LA CAMPESINA

      BISTEC DE TERNERA A LA PLANCHA

      CALAMARES A LA ROMANA

      RIÑONES AL JEREZ

      SARDINAS A LA PLANCHA

POSTRES:

      YOGHOURES VARIADOS

      FRUTA DEL TIEMPO

      NATILLAS O HELADO

PAN, VINO O AGUA O CAÑA DE CERVEZA, POSTRE O
CAFE. TODO INCLUIDO.
OJO: MEDIANAS, CARAJILLOS, REFRESCOS Y TODO
LO DEMAS SE PAGARA APARTE.
(GRAN SURTIDO A LA CARTA)
RESTAURANTE LA OFICINA
"JARDIN III"

Preu: 675 pts

1. Which dish should you order if you want to eat chicken?

   _____

2. Which dish should you order if you want to eat vegetables?

   _____

3. Which dish offers paella?

   _____

4. Which dish offers seafood?

   _____

5. How does this restaurant cook steak?

   _____

6. Could you order ice cream for dessert in this restaurant?

   _____

7. Could you order water or coffee in this restaurant?

   _____

8. Does the restaurant offer any juice?

   _____

9. What would you like to order from this menu?

   _____

Unit 10

A Complete each sentence by writing the name of the appropriate artist.

1. If you like paintings with religious subjects, you might like the artworks of
_____ .

2. If you like seeing pictures of ordinary, simple people, you might enjoy the artworks of
_____ .

3. If you prefer seeing pictures of how rich people used to dress in Spain, you might like the
artworks of _____ .

B Match the artists in column B with the appropriate expressions in column A.

	A			B
1.	*The Water Carrier of Seville*	_____	a.	El Greco
2.	*The Burial of the Count of Orgaz*	_____	b.	Diego Velázquez
3.	*The Parasol*	_____	c.	Francisco de Goya
4.	*Don Manuel Osorio de Zúñiga*	_____		
5.	classicism	_____		
6.	realistic mysticism	_____		
7.	rococo and neobaroque	_____		
8.	spiritual salvation	_____		
9.	human dignity	_____		
10.	social customs	_____		
11.	Seville	_____		
12.	Madrid	_____		
13.	Toledo	_____		
14.	died in 1614	_____		
15.	died in 1828	_____		
16.	died in 1660	_____		

C Having read about the lives, paintings and artistic styles of El Greco, Velázquez and Goya on page 64 of your textbook, decide which artist fits each description.

1. He was born on the isle of Crete.

    _____

2. He was born near Zaragoza.

    _____

3. His successful career began at the age of 20.

    _____

4. He became depressed by the world around him and began to paint people in an ugly way.

    _____

5. His real name is Doménicos Theotokópoulos.

    _____

6. He studied art in Venice, Italy.

    _____

7. He was the royal court artist until his death.

    _____

8. He went to Madrid at 27 and became famous.

    _____

9. He gave life and feeling to all his paintings by using color and light skillfully.

    _____

D Draw each item named.

1. un libro

4. una manzana

2. una casa

5. un tenedor

3. una piña

6. un plato

E **Draw a picture to show what each person is doing.**

1. Tomás come (*is eating*) una naranja.

2. Sara levanta la mano.

3. Luz escribe con un boli.

4. Daniel habla con el cartero.

F Of the four pictures you have studied in this unit, *The Burial of the Count Orgaz, The Water Carrier of Seville, Don Manuel Osorio de Zúñiga* and *The Parasol*, decide which one is your favorite. Your teacher will designate each corner of your classroom as one of these four paintings. Go to the corner that represents your favorite picture. Pair up with a partner. Each of you tells the other why you like this painting the best. Then get together with another pair of students in your corner so that you can tell the new pair why your partner prefers this painting. Finally, a spokesperson from each of the four groups tells the entire class why students from that group prefer that picture.

G *Museos en Barcelona.* Write the letter of each museum next to the appropriate description. Here are some words that you may need to know:

albergará = will house   cera = wax

a
MUSEO PICASSO. Pintura, dibujo, cerámica y obra gráfica representativa de Pablo Picasso y su evolución artística (1881-1957). Ubicado en los palacios góticos de Berenguer Aguilar y Barón de Castellet.
Montcada, 15-19. Tel. 319 63 10.
Horario: de martes a domingo, de 10.00 a 20.00. Cierra los lunes.

b
MUSEO DE ARTE MODERNO. Notables colecciones de arte de los siglos XIX y XX, fundamentalmente de artistas catalanes o vinculados a Cataluña.
Plaça d'Armes (Parque de la Ciutadella). Tel. 319 57 28.
Horario: de martes a sábado de 9.00 a 19.30; domingos y festivos, de 9.00 a 14.00; lunes, de 15.00 a 19.30.

c
FUNDACION JOAN MIRO. Exposición permanente de obras de Joan Miró. Exposiciones temporales de arte contemporáneo.
Plaça Neptú, s/n (Parque de Montjuïc). Tel. 329 19 08.
Horario: de martes a sábado de 11.00 a 19.00 (jueves, hasta las 21.30); domingos y festivos, de 10.30 a 14.30. Cierra los lunes.

d
MUSEO-MONASTERIO DE PEDRALBES. Conjunto arquitectónico, escultórico y pictórico de gran valor histórico-artístico. Próximamente albergará obras de la colección Thyssen-Bornemiza.
Baixada del Monestir 9. Tel. 203 92 82.
Horario: de martes a domingo, de 9.30 a 14.00. Cierra lunes y festivos.

e MUSEO DE LA MUSICA. Colección de instrumentos musicales de todo el mundo desde el siglo XVI al XX. Edificio modernista obra de Puig i Cadafalch.
Av. Diagonal, 373. Tel. 217 11 57.
Horario: de martes a domingo de 9.00 a 14.00. Lunes, cerrado.

f MUSEO ETNOLOGICO. Piezas representativas de las culturas de pueblos de todos los continentes.
Passeig de Santa Madrona, s/n (Parque de Montjuïc). Tel. 424 64 02.
Horario: de martes a sábado de 9.00 a 20.30; domingos y festivos de 9.00 a 14.00. Lunes, de 15.00 a 20.30 horas.

g MUSEO DE CERA. Reproducción de 300 personajes en escenarios de realidad y de ficción, ambientados con proyecciones y efectos sonoros.
Passatge de la Banca, 7 (La Rambla, 4). Tel. 330 94 11.
Horario: todos los días, de 11.30 a 13.30 y de 16.30 a 19.30.

h MUSEO DE ARTE DE CATALUNYA. Alberga la mejor colección del mundo de arte romántico y medieval. Arte catalán y de otras escuelas peninsulares y europeas desde la Edad Media hasta el siglo XVIII.
Palacio Nacional (Parque de Montjuïc). Tel. 423 18 24.
Horario: de martes a domingo, de 9.00 a 14.00 horas. Cierra los lunes.

1. _____ has paintings of Picasso

2. _____ has wax reproductions of 300 people

3. _____ has works from Joan Miró

4. _____ has the best collection of Romanesque and Medieval art

5. _____ has modern art from the twentieth century

6. _____ has a collection of musical instruments

7. _____ will house the collection of Thyssen-Bornemiza

8. _____ has representations from cultures of all continents

H Crucigrama. Complete the following crossword puzzle with information from this unit.

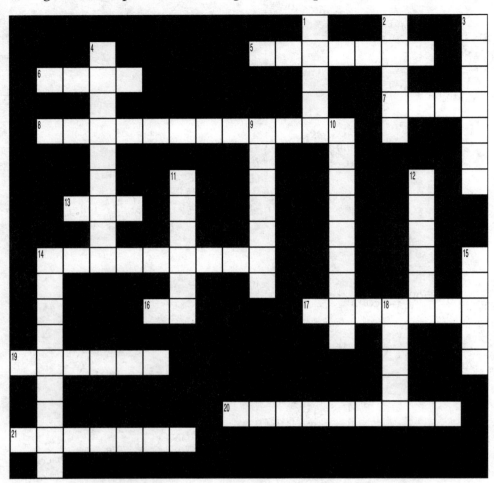

Vertical

1. birthplace of El Greco
2. Velázquez and Goya painted at the...court.
3. Goya was discouraged by the...around him.
4. El Greco's style is....
9. Velázquez was the "father of Spanish...."
10. kind of paintings done by El Greco
11. *The...of the Count of Orgaz*
12. city in Spain where El Greco lived
14. ...*Osorio de Zúñiga*, oil painting
15. ...del Prado, Madrid
18. Catedral de Santo..., Toledo

Horizontal

5. *The...,* painting by Goya
6. artist of the rococo and neobaroque style
7. art
8. *The...of Seville,* painting by Velázquez
13. Many paintings are made with....
14. first name of El Greco
16. ...Greco
17. social...of Spanish peasant life, subject of Goya's paintings
19. capital of Spain
20. first name of Goya
21. Spanish city used in the name of one of Velázquez's paintings

Unit 11

A Match the parts of the body in column B with their English equivalents in column A.

A	B
1. hair _____	a. el pie
2. nose _____	b. la oreja
3. foot _____	c. la rodilla
4. chest _____	d. la cabeza
5. neck _____	e. la nariz
6. elbow _____	f. el pecho
7. ear _____	g. el cuello
8. eye _____	h. el codo
9. knee _____	i. el pelo
10. head _____	j. el ojo

B Odd one out! Circle the letter of the expression that does not belong with the others.

1. a. pie   b. Pasa a la pizarra.   c. codo

2. a. barbilla   b. Escribe.   c. mano

3. a. Lee.   b. frente   c. ojos

4. a. pecho   b. oreja   c. Escucha.

5. a. Habla.   b. dedos del pie   c. boca

C Escribe la letra que falta. *Write the missing letter.*

1. el o____o   6. la car____

2. el die____te   7. la f____ente

3. la ____odilla   8. el estó____ago

4. el cod____   9. la ____ierna

5. la bo____a   10. el pe____o

D Contesta las siguientes preguntas en español.

1. Which part of your body tells you that something is baking in the oven?

   _____

2. What need milk to make them strong?

   _____

3. In order to eat, what do you open?

   _____

4. What bend to help you sit down?

   _____

5. What do you use to throw a ball?

   _____

6. Where would you wear a wedding ring?

   _____

7. Where do women traditionally wear earrings?

   _____

8. Where do women wear lipstick?

   _____

9. Where do you put contact lenses?

   _____

10. Where do women wear makeup?

   _____

E   Complete the sentences with the appropriate body part in Spanish. You will need to know new words:

entre = between
mitad = middle
arriba = above

1. La _____ está entre los ojos.

2. El _____ está entre el cuello y el estómago.

3. El _____ está entre los hombros.

4. El _____ está entre el hombro y la mano.

5. La _____ está en la mitad de la pierna.

6. El _____ está en la mitad del cuerpo.

7. Hay cinco _____ en la mano.

8. Hay treinta y dos _____ en la boca.

9. En la _____ están la nariz, los ojos y la boca.

10. La _____ está arriba de los ojos.

F Crucigrama. Complete the following crossword puzzle with vocabulary from this unit.

Vertical

2. where thinking takes place
4. "...la otra."
5. help you speak
7. lets you see
9. on top of arm
12. chews food
13. "las partes del..."
15. between neck and stomach

Horizontal

1. where food enters the body
3. holds the head up
6. where food is digested
8. identifies fragrances and odors
10. between hand and shoulder
11. used for kneeling
14. used for touching and pointing
15. used for swimming and walking
16. what you put into your shoe
17. lets you hear

G Working in pairs, practice the Spanish names for the parts of the body, using a doll, a teddy bear, a picture of a person or yourselves. Taking turns, each of you should point to a part of the body and ask what it is, and the other should answer.

EJEMPLO: A: ¿Qué es esto?

B: Es el hombro.

H In the space provided draw a person, one section at a time. Working in pairs, your partner announces a part of the body, for example, "el pie," and you draw it. Continue until the picture is completed. You might try drawing a cat or another animal, but you may have to look up some Spanish words, such as tail, paw, etc.

I Sometimes certain parts of your body get injured or ache and need professional attention. Look carefully at the advertisements for Colombian doctors that treat specific parts of the body. Then decide which doctor you should visit if each of the parts of your body that follow hurts. Write the name of the appropriate doctor in the space provided. Here are some words you may need to know:

cardiólogo = cardiologist, heart specialist

neurólogo = neurologist, head specialist

odontólogo = dentist

HECTOR J. HERNANDEZ G.
CARDIOLOGO HEMODINAMISTA
CATETERISMO CARDIACO - CUIDADO INTENSIVO
CLINICA SHAIO
U.I.S. - ESCUELA COLOMBIANA DE MEDICINA
CLINICA METROPOLITANA CONSULT. 702
47 00 07 - 43 24 06
BIPER 43 22 00 - RES. 38 31 70
PROXIMAMENTE CENTRO MEDICO EL BOSQUE CONSULT. 608

LUIS POLO MONTES
U. NACIONAL - BRASIL RIO DE JANEIRO
HOSPITAL MILITAR CENTRAL - SANTA FE DE BOGOTA
INSTITUTO FRANKLIN DELANO ROOSEVELT
CIRUGIA DE ORTOPEDIA Y TRAUMATOLOGIA
COLUMNA - (FIJACION) - FRACTURAS
REEMPLAZOS ARTICULARES
(CAD - RODILLA - HOMBRO)
ORTOPEDIA INFANTIL
CONSULTORIO: Cr. 33 No. 41 - 24 **45 00 71**
RESIDENCIA **34 29 06**
Localizable Permanentemente **43 22 00**

S.O.S. mano
URGENCIAS Y CIRUGIA
ESPECIALIZADA DE LA MANO
Y EL MIEMBRO SUPERIOR
LINEA PERMANENTE DE URGENCIAS
44 36 03   COD. 012
43 27 23
INFORMACION
47 82 46 - 47 01 71
470171 A partir del Segundo Semestre / 92 436038
DRA. PATRICIA ARRIA RADA

DOCTOR MIGUEL
QUINTERO
VILLAMIZAR
Odontólogo USTA
Odontología Integral del
Niño y el Adulto
Dg. 105 No. 105-28 Local 107-108
Frente a la Plaza Satélite del Sur
36 01 64

CIRUGIA ESTETICA
ESPECIALIZADA
REJUVENECIMIENTO FACIAL - NARIZ
CIRUGIA DEL SENO - LIPOSUCCION
MIGUEL REYES GUERRERO
U.I.S. - MEXICO - RIO DE JANEIRO
Cr. 34 No. 44 - 70 . . . . **43 25 60**

DR. LUIS FRANCISCO
GALEANO ARRIETA
OTORRINOLARINGOLOGO
U.I.S. - U. DEL VALLE
• OIDO - NARIZ - GARGANTA - CUELLO
• OTORRINO - PEDIATRIA
• TRAUMA MAXILOFACIAL
CALLE 46 No. 33 - 16 CEFESAN
47 88 47 - 47 82 46
RES: **45 03 38**

FELIX RINCON
DIAZ
U.I.S BUCARAMANGA
UNIVERSIDAD DE MONTPELLIER (FRANCIA)
NEUROLOGO CLINICO
CL. 51 No. 35 - 28 INT. 100 OF. 406
47 50 83
Residencia **47 37 61**
BUSCAPERSONAS **43 22 00**

Dr. HUMBERTO
CASADIEGO
ENFERMEDADES Y CIRUGIA DE LOS
OJOS Y PARPADOS
LENTES INTRAOCULARES
U.I.S. - URUGUAY - ARGENTINA
Cr. 33 No. 48-66 - 47 53 17 - 47 17 49
47 53 17 a partir del Segundo
Semestre/92: 43 70 91

1. nose

   _____

2. eyes

   _____

3. knee

   _____

4. head

   _____

5. hand

   _____

6. neck

   _____

7. heart

   _____

8. shoulder

   _____

9. teeth

   _____

Unit 12

A Match each clothing item in column B with the appropriate description in column A.

	A			B
1.	dressy female attire	_____	a.	blusa
2.	formal male attire	_____	b.	corbata
3.	bedtime or casual attire	_____	c.	bata
4.	worn around the neck	_____	d.	vestido
5.	female attire with a skirt	_____	e.	traje
6.	footwear with a bathrobe	_____	f.	chaqueta
7.	covering for the head	_____	g.	sombrero
8.	short jacket	_____	h.	abrigo
9.	long coat	_____	i.	cinturón
10.	worn to hold up pants	_____	j.	zapatillas

B Odd one out! Circle the letter of the word that does not belong with the others.

1.	a. guantes	b. sombrero	c. pijama
2.	a. zapatos	b. blusa	c. zapatillas
3.	a. pañuelo	b. falda	c. pantalones
4.	a. vestido	b. camisa	c. corbata
5.	a. camisa	b. blusa	c. calcetines

C   Name the article of clothing in Spanish that you wear or use in the following situations.

1. You wear this over your pajamas.   _____

2. You put these on your hands.   _____

3. You use this when you blow your nose.   _____

4. You wear this accessory around your waist.   _____

5. You wear this on your head.   _____

6. You wear these on your feet when you go out.   _____

D   Descifra las palabras.

1. AABT   _____

2. AGSETNU   _____

3. ÑOPEAUL   _____

4. RNINOCUT   _____

5. BOOSERMR   _____

6. ZPOATAS   _____

7. ADFLA   _____

8. OBCARTA   _____

9. LAAN   _____

10. JRTAE   _____

E Find your way through the clothing store. Name the items of clothing you encounter on your way.

_____   _____

_____   _____

_____   _____

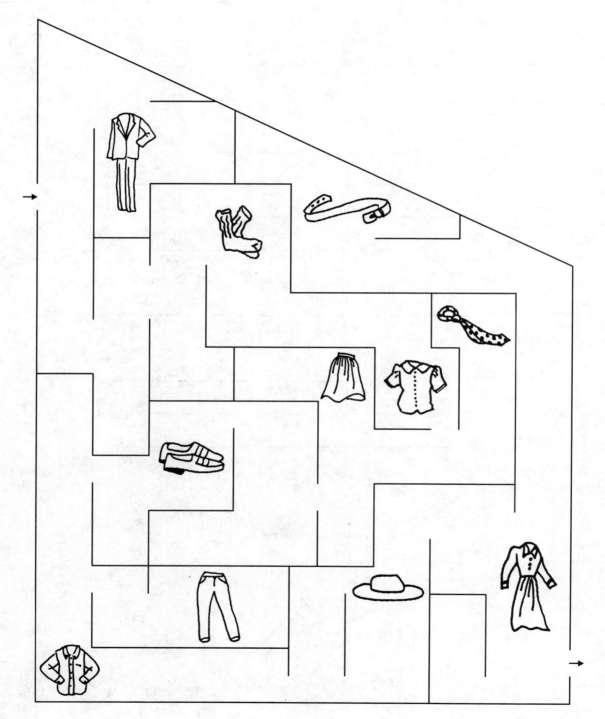

F Sopa de letras. *Wordsearch*. Find and circle the following items of clothing.

1. pañuelo
2. falda
3. sombrero
4. guantes
5. chaqueta

6. vestido de lana
7. cinturones
8. suéteres
9. zapatos
10. abrigo

```
U  R  V  E  G  S  T  A  F  I  D  Ñ  A
S  C  H  A  Q  U  E  T  A  D  O  L  O
U  O  I  O  A  T  B  O  L  A  Ñ  G  Z
E  T  G  N  T  N  P  A  D  L  I  N  A
T  P  U  F  T  E  L  E  A  R  G  U  P
E  N  A  A  E  U  O  R  B  O  U  S  A
R  C  A  Ñ  S  S  R  A  R  E  A  O  T
E  I  D  L  U  I  R  O  T  Ñ  N  B  O
S  O  M  B  R  E  R  O  N  A  T  P  S
A  Q  U  E  E  A  L  E  R  E  E  M  A
Ñ  H  U  S  T  A  F  O  L  D  S  A  Z
V  E  S  T  I  D  O  D  E  L  A  N  A
```

G Who wears what and where? Begin by thinking of five names of occupations in Spanish. Say each occupation and your partner will say what someone who has that job typically wears.

EJEMPLO: **A:** profesor
   B: traje, camisa, corbata, cinturón, calcetines, zapatos

Then it's your partner's turn. He or she thinks of five names of places in Spanish. After he or she says each one, you will say what someone in that location typically wears.

EJEMPLO: **B:** baño
   A: bata, pijama, zapatillas

H While staying at a hotel in Colombia, Sr. and Sra. Vega had the hotel's laundry service clean some of their clothes. Look at the laundry form the Vegas filled out and answer the questions in Spanish. (Prices are given in pesos.) Here are some words that you may need to know:

lavandería = laundry

toalla = towel

traje de baño = bathing suit

SERVICIO DE LAVANDERIA DE LUNES A SABADO

CUENTA HUESPED	HOTEL	SEÑORES	PRECIO	CANTIDAD	
Sr. Vega		CAMISAS	6.000	18.000	3
		CAMISETA	3.500		
		CALZONCILLO	2.800	11.200	4
		CALCETINES (PAR)	2.500		
		PAÑUELO	2.500	5.000	2
		PIJAMA	9.400		
		SHORTS	6.500		
		TRAJE DE BAÑO	6.000		
		PANTALONES	8.000	32.000	4
			SUB-TOTAL		13

CUENTA HUESPED	Hotel	SEÑORAS	PRECIO	CANTIDAD	
Sra. Vega		BLUSA	6.000	12.000	2
		VESTIDO	11.000	11.000	1
		FONDO	4.500		
		CAMISON	9.600		
		BRASSIERE	3.000		
		PANTALETA	3.000		
		PAÑUELO	3.000	9.000	3
		SHORTS	6.500		
		FALDA	6.500	32.500	5
		TRAJE DE BAÑO	7.000	7.000	1
		PANTALONES	8.000		
		FAJAS	5.000		
		MEDIAS	2.500		
		TOALLA BAÑO	7.500	15.000	2
		BATA BAÑO	11.000	11.000	1
IVA INCLUIDO			SUB-TOTAL		15
					28

INSTRUCCIONES ESPECIALES

TOTAL $ 163,700

NOMBRE _Carlos Vega R. y Sra. Vega_
FECHA _04/06_   No. _405_   VALET Bo._____
Precios por ropa de hechura sencilla.

1. What is Sr. Vega's first name?

   _____

2. Which days of the week is the hotel's laundry service open?

   _____

3. How many shirts did Sr. Vega have cleaned?

   _____

4. How many handkerchiefs did Sra. Vega have cleaned?

   _____

5. How many pairs of pants did Sr. Vega have cleaned?

   _____

6. How much did it cost to have Sra. Vega's blouses cleaned?

   _____

7. How much did it cost to have Sra. Vega's towels cleaned?

   _____

8. How much did it cost to have Sra. Vega's bathing suit cleaned?

   _____

9. Did Sra. Vega send her bathrobe to the laundry service?

   _____

10. Did Sr. Vega send a pair of pajamas to the laundry service?

    _____

Unit 13

A Answer each question by circling the appropriate letter. Watch out for times expressed according to the twenty-four-hour system!

1. At what time does the sun rise?

    a. a las seis y dos   b. a las dos y seis

2. At what time does the sun set?

    a. a las dos   b. a las diecinueve horas

3. At what time do you leave for school in the morning?

    a. a las trece horas   b. a las ocho y media

4. At what time are you dismissed from school each day?

    a. a las catorce horas   b. a medianoche

5. At what time does the afternoon movie start?

    a. a las catorce horas   b. a las diez

6. What time would you go stargazing?

    a. a la una   b. a las veintidós horas

B Identify the color generally associated with each item. (En español, por favor.)

1. raspberries   _____

2. rainclouds   _____

3. snowballs   _____

4. sunflowers   _____

5. crows   _____

6. ocean   _____

7. "queso"   _____

8. "leche"   _____

9. "espinacas"   _____

10. "tomates"   _____

Color combinations. Each color on the left is a combination of two others. Do you know what they are? (En español, por favor.)

1. verde = _____ + _____

2. anaranjado = _____ + _____

3. gris = _____ + _____

4. rosado = _____ + _____

5. violeta = _____ + _____

D Write each time using numbers.

1. Son las diez menos cuarto. _____

2. Son las tres y media. _____

3. Son las veinte horas. _____

4. Son las cinco y diecisiete. _____

5. Es la una. _____

6. Es mediodía. _____

7. Es medianoche. _____

8. Son las seis y cuarto. _____

Crucigrama. Complete the following crossword puzzle with vocabulary from this unit.

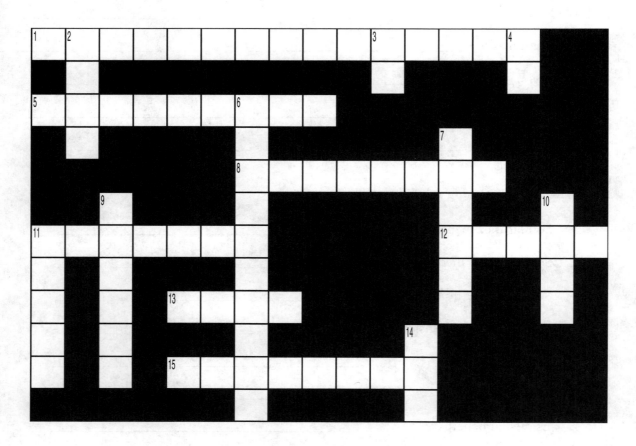

Vertical

2. color of water and sky
3. "¿...qué color es?"
4. "...la una."
6. color of an orange
7. color of clouds and salt
9. light red
10. Black and white make....
11. color of grass in the spring
14. "a...dos y cinco"

Horizontal

1. "...nunca."
5. What time is it?
8. color of lemons
11. color of bluish-red flower
12. color of India ink and pepper
13. color of strawberries and tomatoes
15. time when sun is at highest point in the sky

F At what time do you do certain things? Make up a list of 10 activities you do on a regular basis. Then, working in pairs, your partner chooses one activity from your list and asks you at what time you do that activity. You must answer with a Spanish phrase.

> EJEMPLO: A: At what time do you generally eat supper?
>
> B: *A las seis.*

Your partner should write down the times you say and at the end summarize what you said. Then switch roles.

G Working in pairs, take turns identifying the colors around you. Your partner must find objects of different colors. He or she then says "I see something in this room that is (a certain color)." The color must be said in Spanish. You are to identify the object in Spanish, if you can.

> EJEMPLO: A: I see something in this room that is *amarillo.*
>
> B: *Es un lápiz.*

H Here is a Colombian television schedule for a Sunday in November. Look at the schedule and answer the questions in Spanish. Here are some words that you may need to know:

presenta = presents   empieza = begins
canal = channel   termina = ends

DOMINGO 29 DE NOVIEMBRE

		8:00 A.M.	8:30	9:00	9:30	10:00	10:30	11:00	11:30	12:00
T.V. NACIONAL	UNO	Personajes y Canciones	Buenos Días Bulliciosos		Las Tortugas Ninja	Dominguísimo		El Cóndor		Automan
	A	El Club de las Preguntas	Maxi Mini		Erase una Vez las Américas	El Hechicero		Paraíso		Tasha y la Tierra Perdida
	TRES									
REGIONALES	TELECARIBE	Santa Misa	El Libro Encantado	Rápido Rápido	En la Jugada	Fútbol Italiano			En la Jugada	Estelares del Vallenato
	TELEANTIOQUIA									
	TELEPACIFICO	Santa Misa		Fútbol Italiano					Trans World Sport	

		12:30 P.M.	1:00	1:30	2:00	2:30	3:00	3:30	4:00	4:30
T.V. NACIONAL	UNO	Automan (cont.)	Noticiero NTC	Misión Secreta		El Show de las Estrellas		Ecolombia	Decisiones	
	A	Super Mario Bros	Noticiero Criptón	Guardianes de la Bahía		Mujeres en Acción		No Me lo Cambie		
	TRES									
REGIONALES	TELECARIBE	Estalares del Vallenato (cont.)	Especial: Reinado Nacional de la Belleza		Especial		Domingo Sensacional			Fútbol Nacional
	TELEANTIOQUIA				Luz Verde	MacGyver		Trans World Sport	El Mejor Fútbol del Mundo	
	TELEPACIFICO	Variette			Regionales de Película				Fútbol en Directo: Cuadrangular Final	

		5:00 P.M.	5:30	6:00	6:30	7:00	7:30	8:00	8:30	9:00
T.V. NACIONAL	UNO	Cine Disney				Tarzán	Archivo Secreto	Los Años Maravillosos	Noticiero TV. Hoy	Gran Nocturna: Intriga Tropical
	A	Videos Totalm. Ocultos	La Factura Millonaria	Misión Imposible		Locos Videos	Vuelo Secreto	Dejémonos de Vainas	Noticiero Notivisión	Playa Infernal
	TRES	Mofli, el Ultimo Koala	Fofura	Historias Cortas	Conciertos Latinoamericanos		Noticiero del Deporte	Historia en Desarrollo		News File
REGIONALES	TELECARIBE	Fútbol Nacional (cont.)	Ruta del Saber	Especial	Oro Puro	Heredad	Reportaje Mundial	NotiCaribe	Tiempo de Amor	CronoDeportes
	TELEANTIOQUIA	El Mejor Fútbol del Mundo (cont.)		Especial: Los Colombianos...	Directísimo	El Doctor Cándido Pérez	Los Animales y el Hombre	Noticias Fin de Semana	Señora	Fashion TV.
	TELEPACIFICO	Fútbol en Directo (cont.)		Estrellas del Pacífico		Señora		Noticiero NotiPacífico	Tenis Club	Videos Internacionales

		9:30 P.M.	10:00	10:30	11:00	11:30	12:00	12:30	1:00 A.M.	1:30
T.V. NACIONAL	UNO	Gran Nocturna: Intriga... (cont.)	Cinema Uno				Cierre			
	A	Playa Infernal (cont.)	Cinema A				Cierre			
	TRES	Cine Colcultura			Visión Visión	Cierre				
REGIONALES	TELECARIBE	Grandes Miniseries		News File	Cierre					
	TELEANTIOQUIA	Modos y Moda/ Música 98.9	La Película de las 9: Cleopatra (2a. Parte)				Cierre			
	TELEPACIFICO	Videos Internes. (cont.)	Serie del Domingo: Vientos de Guerra		Cierre					

1. ¿Qué presenta Telecaribe a las ocho y treinta A.M.?

   _____

2. ¿Qué presenta el canal Uno a las tres y media P.M.?

   _____

3. ¿Qué presenta el canal Uno a las siete P.M.?

   _____

4. ¿Qué presenta el canal A a las once P.M.?

   _____

5. ¿Qué presenta Telepacífico a las nueve y cuarto A.M.?

   _____

6. ¿Qué presenta el canal Uno al mediodía?

   _____

7. ¿A qué hora empieza el programa "Noticiero Criptón" en el canal A?

   _____

8. ¿A qué hora empieza el programa "Oro puro" en Telecaribe?

   _____

9. ¿A qué hora termina el programa "Señora" en Teleantioquia?

   _____

10. ¿A qué hora termina el programa "Cinema Uno" en el canal Uno?

   _____

Unit 14

 Match the musician in column B with the appropriate musical work in column A.

	A			**B**
1.	*El sombrero de tres picos*	_____	a.	Antonio Soler
2.	*Et vitam venturi*	_____	b.	Juan Crisóstomo Arriaga
3.	*Fantasía bética*	_____	c.	Manuel de Falla
4.	*Sonatas for the Harpsichord*	_____		
5.	*Quartets for Strings*	_____		
6.	*La vida breve*	_____		
7.	*Symphony in D*	_____		

Circle the letter of the correct answer.

1. Who did not write an opera?

    a. Soler   b. Arriaga   c. De Falla

2. Who was a priest?

    a. De Falla   b. Soler   c. Arriaga

3. Whose music was very similar to Mozart's?

    a. Arriaga's   b. De Falla's   c. Soler's

4. Who won a national honor?

    a. Soler   b. Arriaga   c. De Falla

5. Who played the harpsichord and the organ?

    a. De Falla   b. Arriaga   c. Soler

6. Who had a lot in common with Soler?

    a. Bach   b. Mozart   c. Copeland

7. Who lived around the same time as De Falla?

    a. Vivaldi   b. Ravel   c. Beethoven

8. Who is considered the best classical musician from Spain?

    a. De Falla   b. Soler   c. Arriaga

9. Who is considered the best baroque musician from Spain?

    a. De Falla   b. Arriaga   c. Soler

10. Who wrote music for the stage as well as the orchestra?

    a. Soler   b. De Falla   c. Arriaga

C Write the name of the musician who fits each description.

1. He studied music in Paris.

   _____

2. He studied music in Madrid.

   _____

3. He knew how to build organs.

   _____

4. He wrote an opera at the age of 12.

   _____

5. He was born in Cádiz.

   _____

6. He was both a priest and a composer.

   _____

D Descifra las palabras.

1. GARIARA   _____

2. NOIVLI   _____

3. RSICHHDOARP _____

4. NAGOR   _____

5. TALBEL   _____

E Match the Spanish name of the musical instrument in column B with its corresponding description in column A.

A		B
1. You traditionally hear this during religious services.	_____	a. el clarinete
2. This instrument is like a long tube and has a high-pitched sound.	_____	b. el violín
3. You beat this with sticks.	_____	c. la trompeta
4. This woodwind instrument needs a reed.	_____	d. el órgano
5. You play this with a bow.	_____	e. la batería
6. This instrument plays reveille, a military wake up call.	_____	f. la flauta
7. Country singers often play this.	_____	g. la guitarra

F Sopa de letras. *Wordsearch.* Find and circle the following words found in this unit.

1. Baroque
2. Vivaldi
3. Bach
4. Soler
5. sonatas
6. organ
7. ballet
8. Mozart
9. Arriaga
10. quartet
11. De Falla
12. La vida breve
13. opera
14. classical
15. concertos

```
S B A A U C L I F A D E L V
O E R M S O L E R T O H A B
N R O O Q A A A L E A C R G
A Q G Z L V V L S R R I R A
T U B A C H I E R S E S I D
A A S R N D D L B U I D A E
S R A T L T A A Q A L C G F
C T A E E R B O S A A R A A
P E O L R B R A V T U T N L
L T L L A A E I O Q E O C L
E A E V B I V D T O P E R A
B V C O N C E R T O S R C E
```

The Spanish city of Valencia hosts several music festivals. Look at the program for the Fall Festival *(Festival de Otoño)* and answer the questions that follow. Here are some words that you may need to know:

fecha = date
estreno = premier
título = title

obra = work
director = conductor

Festival de Otoño

Fecha:		Orquesta:	Intérpretes:	Compositor:	Título de la obra:	Precio:
16 OCTUBRE VIERNES 20.15 HORAS	1	Orquesta de Valencia	Vicente Zarzo, trompa María Rosa Calvo Manzano, arpa Manuel Galduf, director	Heitor Villalobos Rafael Talens Xavier Montsalvatge Alberto Ginastera	Bacchiana Brasileira nº 1 Concierto para trompa y orquesta* (homenaje a Miguel Falomir) Concierto para arpa y orquesta Danzas del Ballet "Estancia" * Estreno absoluto	1.000/500
20 OCTUBRE MARTES 20.15 HORAS	2	Coro de Valencia English Chamber Orchestra	Enriqueta Tarrés, soprano Liliana Bizineche, mezzo-soprano Andrew Burden, tenor Roderick Williams, barítono Miriam Fried, violín Leopold Hager, director	Felix Mendelssohn Joseph Haydn	Las Hébridas, Obertura, op. 26 Concierto para violín y orquesta en mi menor, op. 64 Misa Hob XXII: 9 en do mayor, Misa in Tempore Belli "Paukenmesse"	2.550/1.250
24 OCTUBRE MIERCOLES 20.15 HORAS	3	Orquesta Filarmónica de Liege y de la Comunidad Francesa	Pierre Bartholomee, director	Darius Milhaud Claude Debussy Cesar Franck	Serenata, op. 62 El Mar Sinfonía en re menor	1.000/500
30 OCTUBRE VIERNES 20.15 HORAS	4	Orquesta de Valencia BBC Symphony Chorus	Gwendolyn Bradley, soprano Robert Tear, tenor Simon Estes, bajo Manuel Galduf, director	Joseph Haydn	La Creación	1.500/750
8 NOVIEMBRE DOMINGO 19.30 HORAS	5	Orquesta de la Radio Bávara	Lorin Maazel, director	Richard Strauss	Así habló Zartustra Suite Rosenkavalier Till Eulenspiegel	4.000/2.000
13 NOVIEMBRE VIERNES 20.15 HORAS	6	Orquesta de Valencia	Lazar Berman, piano Georgy Dimitrov, director	Felix Mendelssohn Eduard Grieg Igor Stravinski	"Ruy Blas" obertura en do menor, op. 95 Concierto en la menor para piano y orquesta, op. 16 Suite del ballet "Petruchka"	1.500.750
15 NOVIEMBRE DOMINGO 19.30 HORAS	7	Orquesta Filarmónica de Rotterdam	Bruno Leonardo Gelber, piano Jeffrey Tate, director	Hendrik Andriesen Franz Schubert Johannes Brahms	Estudio Sinfónico Sinfonía nº 2 en si bemol mayor Concierto para piano nº 1 en re menor	2.500/1.250
18 NOVIEMBRE MIERCOLES 20.15 HORAS	8	Norddeutscher Rundfunk Hamburg	María Joao Pires, piano John Eliot Gardiner, director	Robert Schumann	Manfred, obertura, op. 115 Concierto para piano y orquesta en la mayor, op. 54 Sinfonía nº 3 en mi bemol mayor, op. 38	4.000/2.000
26 NOVIEMBRE JUEVES 20.15 HORAS	9	Teresa Berganza	Teresa Berganza, mezzo-soprano Alvarez Parejo, piano	Recital Rossini	Concierto a beneficio de la Asociación Valenciana contra el SIDA	3.000/1.500
27 NOVIEMBRE VIERNES 20.15 HORAS	10	Orquesta de Valencia	Ernesto Bitetti, guitarra Enrique García Asensio, director	Joaquín Rodrigo Eduardo López Chavarri Leo Brower Igor Stravinski	Adagio para instrumentos de viento Concierto para guitarra y orquesta* Concierto para guitarra y orquesta nº 3 El pájaro de fuego (1914) * Estreno absoluto	1.500/750

1. What is the date of the first concert of this festival?

    _____

2. At what time does this concert start?

    _____

3. Which orchestra will perform on November 13?

    _____

4. Which orchestra will perform on November 15?

    _____

5. Whose music is going to be played on November 8?

    _____

6. How many premier performances are there in this festival?

    _____

7. Who will play the violin on October 20?

    _____

8. Who will play the piano on November 26?

    _____

9. Who will play the guitar on November 27?

    _____

10. What is the title of the musical work being performed on October 30?

    _____

11. Who will conduct the concert on October 24?

    _____

12. Which concert would you like to attend?

    _____

H Interview your partner about his or her musical tastes. Ask your partner the following questions and note his or her answers. Then reverse roles so that your partner interviews you.

1. What is your favorite type of music?

   _____

   _____

2. Who are your favorite male and female singers?

   _____

   _____

3. Who is your favorite group?

   _____

   _____

4. Can you name a singer or group from outside the U.S.?

   _____

   _____

5. Have you ever seen any singers or groups in concert? If so, which singer(s) or group(s)?

   _____

   _____

6. Do you play any musical instruments? If so, which one(s)?

   _____

   _____

Unit 15

A Match Column B with Column A.

A		B
1. Nieva.	_____	a. sun
2. ¿Qué tiempo hace?	_____	b. season
3. primavera	_____	c. How's the weather?
4. frío	_____	d. It's snowing.
5. mal	_____	e. windy
6. sol	_____	f. bad
7. viento	_____	g. cold
8. estación	_____	h. spring
9. Relampaguea.	_____	i. It's sunny.
10. Hace sol.	_____	j. There's lightning.

B Complete logically the following sentences to explain your reasons for advising travelers going to different places about what to pack or do.

1. warm clothing

   En invierno en Madrid hace _____ .

2. lightweight clothing

   En verano en México, D.F. hace _____ .

3. coat and hat

   En otoño en Barcelona hace _____ y hace

   _____ .

4. umbrella

   En verano en Veracruz _____ .

5. ski suit

   En invierno en Portillo, Chile _____ .

6. swimsuit

   En verano en Acapulco hace _____ .

7. light jacket

   En primavera en Buenos Aires, Argentina hace _____ .

8. sunscreen

   En verano en España hace _____ .

C ¿En qué estación estamos? Name in Spanish the season when the following weather is typical.

1. Hace buen tiempo. _____

2. Hace viento y llueve. _____

3. Nieva. _____

4. Hace viento y hace frío. _____

5. Está húmedo. _____

D Name in Spanish the season when the following events usually take place.

1. Some birds fly south.

    _____

2. Some animals hibernate.

    _____

3. It feels better to be in the shade than in the sun.

    _____

4. The air gets warmer and the snow starts to melt.

    _____

5. You carve pumpkins.

    _____

6. Trees begin to bud.

    _____

E Write a sentence in Spanish that describes the weather associated with each of the following items.

1. lawn chair

    _____

2. ice skates

    _____

3. lilacs

    _____

4. snowsuit

    _____

5. rake

    _____

6. perspiration

    _____

7. atmospheric electricity

    _____

8. noise in the sky

    _____

F Make a list of as many Spanish sentences as you can that describe the weather. Then working in pairs, say each sentence as a clue for your partner. He or she will say the name of the appropriate season in Spanish and also will say, if possible, what he or she is wearing.

EJEMPLO: **A:** Hace frío.
            B: El invierno. Llevo guantes, sombrero y abrigo.

After you have said each of your sentences, reverse roles. Now your partner gives you clues and you tell the season and what you're wearing.

G Find your way through the seasons. Using the pictures as cues, name the weather conditions you encounter on your way.

_____   _____
_____   _____
_____   _____
_____   _____
                                    _____

H *¿Qué tiempo hace?* Here is a map showing today's weather conditions in Spain and temperatures in other parts of the world. Look carefully at this weather report, read the statements that follow and decide whether they are true *(verdad)* or false *(falso)*. Write V or F in the spaces provided. (Temperatures in Spain are measured in centigrade. To convert a temperature measured in centigrade to Fahrenheit, multiply the temperature by 9, divide it by 5 and then add 32. [Example: 20°C X 9 ÷ 5 + 32 = 68°F] Also, the letters printed after the names of the cities in the temperature chart refer to the weather conditions listed below the chart.) Here are some words that you may need to know:

cubierto = cloudy   **chubazcos** = heavy rain
tormenta = electrical storm   **llovizna** = drizzle

EL TIEMPO

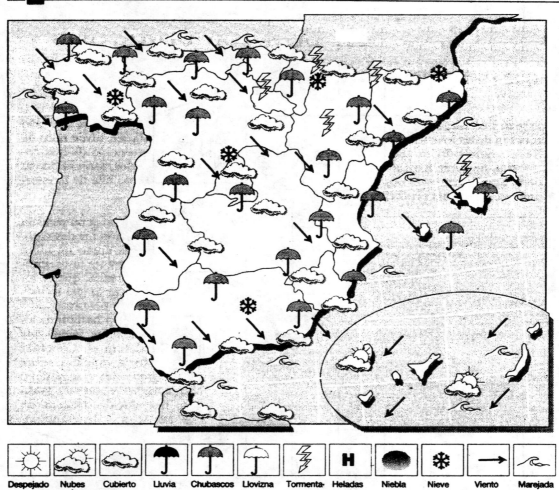

ESPAÑA		MÁX.	MÍN.			MÁX.	MÍN.
Albacete	P	16	9	Madrid	V	20	12
Alicante	P	27	15	Mahón	P	22	11
Almería	D	25	13	Málaga	c	25	16
Ávila	P	15	9	Melilla	D	23	17
Badajoz	P	22	13	Murcia	D	26	11
Barcelona	P	22	13	Orense	P	16	13
Bilbao	P	20	15	Oviedo	P	16	13
Burgos	P	11	8	Palencia	P	12	8
Cáceres	P	23	11	Palma	P	23	19
Cádiz	D	22	17	Palmas, Las	c	25	20
Castellón	P	23	15	Pamplona	P	16	12
Ceuta	D	22	17	Pontevedra	P	16	7
Ciudad Real	P	19	11	Salamanca	P	15	10
Córdoba	P	17	12	San Sebastián	P	18	14
Coruña, La	V	15	13	S. C. Tenerife	c	25	19
Cuenca	P	15	8	Santander	P	18	14
Gerona	P	21	12	Santiago de C.	P	13	10
Gijón	V	14	12	Segovia	P	14	9
Granada	P	16	5	Sevilla	A	22	14
Guadalajara	P	19	8	Soria	P	11	6
Huelva	A	22	13	Tarragona	P	22	16
Huesca	P	14	10	Teruel	P	16	9
Ibiza	Q	24	14	Toledo	P	20	13
Jaén	P	18	12	Valencia	P	23	16
Lanzarote	A	23	20	Valladolid	P	13	10
León	P	10	8	Vigo	P	15	10
Lérida	P	19	12	Vitoria	P	15	10
Logroño	P	16	9	Zamora	P	14	10
Lugo	P	12	7	Zaragoza	P	21	16

EXTRANJERO		MÁX.	MÍN.			MÁX.	MÍN.
Amsterdam	P	16	10	México *	D	18	9
Atenas	D	28	20	Miami *	D	31	25
Berlín	Q	21	14	Moscú	F	3	0
Bruselas	P	14	10	Nueva York *	D	18	13
Buenos Aires *	P	18	10	Oslo	Q	15	7
Cairo, El	D	30	14	París	P	17	14
Estocolmo	D	9	3	Rabat	D	22	14
Francfort	P	15	13	R. de Janeiro *	Q	31	18
Ginebra	P	14	10	Roma	Q	26	18
Lisboa	P	18	16	Tokio *	Q	21	19
Londres	P	11	7	Viena	Q	18	10

A, agradable / **C,** mucho calor / **c,** calor / **D,** despejado / **F,** mucho frío / **t,** frío /**H,** heladas / **N,** nevadas / **P,** lluvioso / **Q,** cubierto / **s,** tormentas / **T,** templado / **v,** vientos fuertes.

1. The maximum temperature in Madrid is 12°C. _____

2. It's windy in Madrid. _____

3. The minimum temperature in Barcelona is 45°F. _____

4. It's raining in Barcelona. _____

5. It's snowing in some parts of northeastern Spain. _____

6. It's sunny in southern Spain. _____

7. In general, it's cloudy and rainy in Spain. _____

8. Northeastern Spain is experiencing electrical activity. _____

9. It's warm in Málaga. _____

10. The maximum temperature in Mexico is 18°F. _____

11. It's very cold in Berlin. _____

12. It's cloudy in Vienna. _____

Unit 16

A Match Column B with Column A.

A		B
1. birthday	_____	a. fiesta
2. today	_____	b. fin de semana
3. week	_____	c. mañana
4. day	_____	d. ayer
5. month	_____	e. cumpleaños
6. school day	_____	f. día escolar
7. tomorrow	_____	g. mes
8. weekend	_____	h. hoy
9. yesterday	_____	i. semana
10. holiday	_____	j. día

B Rearrange the days of the week in the usual sequence. Start with the Spanish word for Monday.

sábado	jueves	domingo	miércoles
viernes	martes	lunes	

1. _____

2. _____

3. _____

4. _____

5. _____

6. _____

7. _____

C Complete each sentence with a Spanish word.

1. If today is "miércoles," tomorrow is " _____ ."

2. If "ayer" was Saturday, " _____ " is Monday.

3. If this month is "diciembre," next month is " _____ ."

4. If the day before yesterday was "jueves," today is " _____ ."

5. If next month is "octubre," this month is " _____ ."

D Write in Spanish the appropriate day of the week or month of the year according to the cues.

1. the day and month when people play jokes   _____

2. the month of Independence Day   _____

3. the month when you send valentines   _____

4. the day honoring the Roman god of war   _____

5. the day honoring the Roman goddess of love   _____

6. the month of Halloween   _____

7. the month when people celebrate Christmas   _____

8. the month when people celebrate Mother's Day   _____

9. the day honoring the moon god   _____

10. the day honoring "the Lord"   _____

E Write the following dates in Spanish. Follow the model.

EJEMPLO: Thursday, February 28
            jueves, el 28 de febrero

1. Saturday, June 6   _____

2. Wednesday, October 13   _____

3. Sunday, December 19   _____

4. Friday, May 21   _____

5. Tuesday, August 7   _____

F Fairs are very popular in Latin American countries. Look at the following calendar of fairs in Colombia and answer the questions that follow *en español*. Here are some words that you may need to know:

feria = fair
hogar = home
flores = flowers

EVENTOS QUE MULTIPLICAN SUS NEGOCIOS

Haga suya la experiencia de Corferias y programe desde ya, su participación en los certámenes de mayor éxito comercial.

CALENDARIO FERIAL

- **COLOMBIAN SHOES AND LEATHER GOODS FAIR**
  Es el evento que reune en un solo sitio a los mejores productores nacionales e internacionales de artículos de cuero y calzado para exportación. **En asocio con ASOCUEROS, CORNICAL Y FEDECURTIDORES.**
  Febrero 24-27

- **VITRINA TURISTICA DE ANATO**
  Es el certamen especializado más importante del sector turístico que se realiza en Colombia, con la presencia de los agentes de viajes, oficinas de turismo internacional, transportadores, servicios, hoteles y restaurantes.
  En asocio con ANATO.
  Marzo 3-5

- **VI FERIA INTERNACIONAL DEL LIBRO**
  Es la cita cultural y comercial más importante del año, entre lectores, editores, importadores y famosos autores de varios países. Mexico país invitado de honor. **En asocio con LA CAMARA COLOMBIANA DEL LIBRO**
  Abril 21-Mayo 3

- **II EXPOCONSTRUCCION Y EXPODISEÑO**
  Es el evento con carácter internacional que reune en un solo recinto los productos, materiales, equipos y avances tecnológicos de la construcción y el diseño arquitectónico, industrial y visual. **En asocio con CAMACOL Y PRODISEÑO**
  Mayo 13-23

- **EXPOMILITAR**
  Gran exhibición de la dotación militar colombiana. Con la participación de las empresas proveedoras de las fuerzas militares. **En asocio con EL EJERCITO DE COLOMBIA**
  Mayo 28-Junio 7

- **GONDOLA**
  Encuentro de los supermercados y almacenes por departamento. **En asocio con FENALCO NACIONAL.**
  Junio 9-11

- **EXPOPARTES**
  Reune productores y representantes nacionales e internacionales de las mejores casas de piezas para automotores. **En asocio con ASOPARTES.**
  Junio 15-19

- **IX AGROEXPO**
  Es la feria más importante de América Latina, con lo último en maquinaria agrícola, salones especializados del sector, además de una destacada exposición ganadera, equina y de especies menores.
  Julio 14-25

- **COLOMBIAN SHOES AND LEATHER GOODS FAIR**
  En asocio con ASOCUEROS, CORNICAL Y FEDECURTIDORES
  Agosto 4-7

- **III EXPOSALUD**
  Es el evento que reune a fabricantes e importadores, congregados entorno a los avances científicos en equipos médicos, odontológicos y hospitalarios. **Con auspicio de LA ACADEMIA NACIONAL DE MEDICINA.**
  Agosto 24-29

- **PROFLORA**
  Es la feria internacional de las flores, donde se resalta la imagen de la floricultura colombiana. **Organizada por ASOCOLFLORES**
  Septiembre 1-5

- **X FERIA DEL HOGAR**
  Certamen con el atractivo de venta directa al público de bienes de consumo nacionales e importados.
  Septiembre 17-Octubre 3

- **JUVENALIA**
  Festival de la infancia y la juventud recoge y divulga la inquietud juvenil a través de sus expositores; cuyos productos están directamente relacionados con el público infantil y juvenil, nuestros invitados de honor.
  Septiembre 17-Octubre 3

- **EXPOCIENCIA**
  En el marco de la apertura económica es la muestra de los últimos avances científicos y tecnológicos a nivel nacional e internacional. **En asocio con LA ASOCIACION COLOMBIANA PARA EL AVANCE DE LA CIENCIA.**
  Octubre 7-15

- **XII COMPUEXPO-SOFTWARE II TELEXPO**
  Es la feria internacional especializada que pone al servicio de Colombia lo último en computadores, programas y equipos de oficina. **En asocio con ACIS y ACUC**
  Octubre 21-28

- **EXPOENERGIA (MINAS, PETROLEOS, ENERGIA ELECTRICA)**
  Amplia el horizonte económico del sector en los cinco continentes, con equipos, tecnología y nuevas inversiones.
  Noviembre 3-7

- **ANDIGRAFICA 93**
  Feria Internacional de la Industria Gráfica. **En asocio con ANDIGRAF**
  Noviembre 16-21

- **FERIA INTERNACIONAL DEL AUTOMOVIL (SALON NAUTICO Y AEREO)**
  Muestra comercial y deportiva que exhibe los últimos modelos de automóviles, motos, lanchas y accesorios.
  Noviembre 25-Diciembre 5

- **III EXPOARTESANIAS**
  Con lo más representativo en artesanías colombianas y de otros países. **En asocio con ARTESANIAS DE COLOMBIA**
  Diciembre 10-19

Carrera 40 No 22C - 67 · Conm: 2440100 al 244 0118 · Telex: 44553 · Telefax 2688469
Cables FIB Santafé de Bogotá, D.C. · Colombia.

CB Camara de Comercio

Avianca

CORFERIAS

1.   In what month is the computer fair?

   _____

2.   When does the home fair begin?

   _____

3.   When does the flower fair begin?

   _____

4.   When does the tourist fair begin?

   _____

5.   In what months can you attend the shoes and leather goods fair?

   _____

6.   When does the automobile fair end?

   _____

7.   In what months is the international book fair?

   _____

8.   How many fairs can you attend in August?

   _____

9.   How many fairs can you attend in October?

   _____

10.   Which fair can you go to on May 28?

   _____

11.   Which fair can you go to on August 24?

   _____

12.   Which fair would you like to attend? When does it begin?

   _____

   _____

Descifra las palabras.

1. RISEVEN   _____

2. ORENE   _____

3. ÑAANAM   _____

4. LOCEMERIS   _____

5. CHEAF   _____

6. EVUJES   _____

7. STOGAO   _____

8. ANMESA   _____

9. TECOBUR   _____

10. BOADAS   _____

 With your classmates play "Birthday Lineup" in Spanish. In this game all students will line up in the chronological order of their dates of birth. Begin by asking one classmate his or her birthday.

EJEMPLO: A: ¿Cuándo es tú cumpleaños?

B: Mi cumpleaños es el dos de febrero.

Then depending on when your birthday is, arrange yourself to the right or left of this person. You will need to ask as many classmates as possible their dates of birth in order to know if you should stand in line to the right or left of them. At the end when everyone is lined up in the correct birth order, each of you will say in turn your date of birth so that the entire class can check the accuracy of the lineup.

Unit 17

A Match the authors in column B with the appropriate literary work in column A.

A		B
1. *La madre naturaleza*	_____	a. Emilia Bazán
2. *Rimas*	_____	b. Rubén Darío
3. *Nada*	_____	c. Miguel de Cervantes
4. *Azul*	_____	d. Carmen Laforet
5. *Don Quijote de la Mancha*	_____	e. Gustavo Adolfo Bécquer
6. *La isla y los demonios*	_____	
7. *Cantos de vida y esperanza*	_____	
8. *Los pazos de Ulloa*	_____	
9. *Novelas ejemplares*	_____	
10. *La mujer nueva*	_____	

B A literary work may be a play, a novel, a story, a dramatic poem, a lyric poem, etc. It may appear also as a collection of poetry or stories. Can you identify each work below? Of what type of literature is each an example?

1. *Don Quijote* _____

2. *Azul* _____

3. *La madre naturaleza* _____

4. *Rimas* _____

5. *La mujer nueva* _____

6. *Oda a Roosevelt* _____

7. *Nada* _____

8. *La isla y los demonios* _____

C Match the literary works in column B with the conflicts in column A.

	A			**B**
1.	heredity vs. environment	_____	a.	poems by Bécquer
2.	naturalism vs. spiritualism	_____	b.	*Don Quijote*
3.	political freedom vs. political oppression	_____	c.	*Los pazos de Ulloa*
4.	chivalry vs. dishonor	_____	d.	*Nada*
5.	imprisonment vs. escape	_____	e.	*Oda a Roosevelt*

D Write the name of the author that fits each description.

1. She promoted the cause of women's rights.

   _____

2. He often worked with his brother.

   _____

3. He was once a prisoner of pirates.

   _____

4. He was also a journalist.

   _____

5. She studied law for a time.

   _____

6. She was a child prodigy.

   _____

7. He was influenced by the French poets.

   _____

8. He lost the use of his left hand at the battle of Lepanto.

   _____

9. She was only thirteen when her mother died.

   _____

10. He died in poverty.

   _____

E Name the city or geographical area where each writer was born.

1. Rubén Darío

   _____

2. Carmen Laforet

   _____

3. Gustavo Bécquer

   _____

4. Emilia Bazán

   _____

5. Miguel de Cervantes

   _____

F What kind of books do you like to read? Decide if you prefer mysteries, adventure stories, science fiction or romance novels. Your teacher will designate each corner of your classroom as one of these four kinds of books. Go to the corner that represents your favorite. Pair up with a partner. Each of you tells the other why you like these books, the last book of this kind you read, its author and something about the plot. Then get together with another pair of students in your corner so that you can tell the new pair what your partner has told you. Finally, a spokesperson from each of the four groups tells the entire class something about what students from that group like to read.

Imagine that you are looking for a good book to read in Spanish. You consult the monthly list of the 10 best-sellers to see what is available. Answer the questions that follow based on the list. Here are some words that you may need to know:

editorial = publisher

posición anterior = previous ranking

LOS LIBROS MAS VENDIDOS

Compilación y notas:
Alonso Aristizábal

Fecha de encuesta:
última semana de julio

FICCION					
Posición actual	**Título**	**Autor**	**Editorial**	**Posición anterior**	**Meses en lista**
1. LA INMORTALIDAD		Milan Kundera	Tusquets	1	4
2. EL PENDULO DE FOUCAULT		Umberto Eco	Alianza Colombia	2	9
3. LA CASA DE LAS DOS PALMAS		Mejía Vallejo	Planeta	3	13
4. DE PARTE DE LA PRINCESA MUERTA		Kenizé Mourad	Arango Editores	4	10
5. MAS GRANDE QUE EL AMOR		Dominique Lapierre	Planeta	—	1
6. LA INVITADA DE HONOR		Irving Wallace	Planeta	—	1
7. SINFONIA DESDE EL NUEVO MUNDO		Germán Espinosa	Planeta	9	2
8. EL LABERINTO		Larry Collins	Plaza	—	1
9. LA CASA RUSIA		John Lecarré	Plaza	10	8
10. OTRAS HISTORIAS DE BALANDU		Mejía Vallejo	Intermedio	—	1

1. What is the name of this week's best-selling book? Who is the author?

   _____

   _____

2. What was this book's ranking last month? How many months has it been on the list?

   _____

   _____

3. Which book has been on the list for the longest time? How long?

   _____

   _____

4. Which books are on the list for the first time this month?

   _____

   _____

5. What publisher has published four of these best-sellers?

   _____

   _____

6. Which two books were ranked higher this month than they were last month?

   _____

   _____

7. Which book would you like to read? Why?

   _____

   _____

H Crucigrama. Complete the following crossword puzzle with information from this unit.

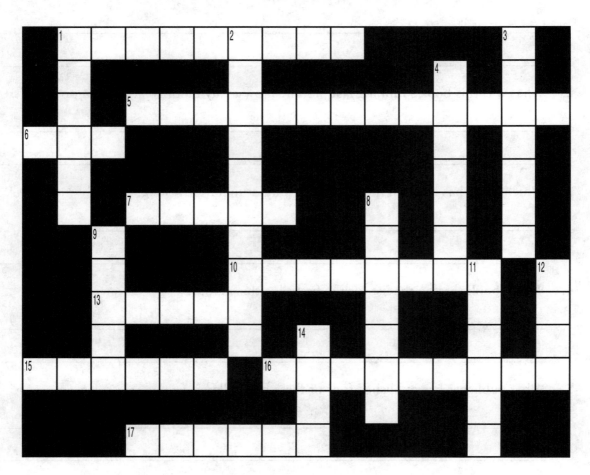

Vertical

1. ...Darío, Nicaragua
2. Bazán introduced "..." into her novels.
3. Carmen...
4. ...*ejemplares* by Cervantes
8. Emilia Bazán's favorite region of Spain
9. journalist and poet of Nicaragua (last name)
11. *Don Quijote de la*...by Cervantes
12. Rubén Darío's first book of poems
14. novel by Laforet that won Spain's highest honor

Horizontal

1. Spain's most famous novelist
5. ...Bécquer
6. ...*a Roosevelt* by Darío
7. Emilia...
10. theme in Bécquer's poetry
13. collection of romantic poems by Bécquer
15. ...*profanas* by Darío
16. *Don Quijote de la Mancha* is a...novel.
17. Rubén Darío's hometown

Unit 18

 A Match each English expression in column B with its Spanish equivalent in column A.

A		B
1. bicicleta	_____	a. to dance
2. partido	_____	b. beach
3. montar a caballo	_____	c. to ski
4. fiesta	_____	d. bike
5. bailar	_____	e. to read
6. playa	_____	f. museum
7. leer	_____	g. party
8. nadar	_____	h. game
9. esquiar	_____	i. to horseback ride
10. museo	_____	j. to swim

B Select a statement from the box to match the word cues.

Voy al partido.	Voy a la playa.
Voy a la fiesta.	Voy al museo.

1. (balloons, music and noisemakers)

   _____

2. (a soccer ball)

   _____

3. (a painting)

   _____

4. (a sand bucket, a shovel and a seashell)

   _____

C Complete each sentence with a word from the box.

---

noche   **encanta**   picnic   **conmigo**

música

bailar   **básquetbol**   también

---

1. Juego al _____ .

2. Me gusta _____ .

3. Mañana hay un _____ .

4. ¿Quieres ir _____ ?

5. ¿Vas a la fiesta esta _____ ?

6. Yo, _____ .

7. Va a haber _____ .

8. Me _____ bailar.

D Circle the letter of the most appropriate answer to each question.

1. ¿Adónde vas tú esta noche?

    a. Me gusta leer.

    b. ¡Yo también!

    c. Voy al partido.

2. ¿Adónde vas tú hoy?

    a. Voy a la exhibición de Goya.

    b. Claro.

    c. Hace calor.

3. ¿Qué deportes haces tú?

    a. En la playa.

    b. Juego al volibol.

    c. Para ver el partido.

4. ¿Dónde hay un picnic mañana?

    a. En la playa.

    b. Son las tres.

    c. Me encanta leer.

5. ¿Quieres ir conmigo a la fiesta?

    a. Me gusta esquiar.

    b. Juego al volibol.

    c. Sí. Me encanta bailar.

6. ¿Vas a la fiesta esta noche?

    a. ¿Verdad?

    b. Claro.

    c. Me gusta el Museo del Prado.

E Descifra las palabras.

1. AQEISUR _____

2. TIFASE _____

3. SATEBBUQOL _____

4. SCIMAU _____

5. DRNAA _____

6. EUMSO _____

7. NOMATR _____

8. OTUFBL _____

9. ALYPA _____

10. ESIBLOB _____

F Sopa de letras. *Wordsearch*. Find and circle the following items found in this unit.

1. fiesta
2. museo
3. playa
4. partido
5. volibol

6. fútbol
7. deportes
8. tenis
9. básquetbol
10. béisbol

```
D  B  U  D  Q  L  O  E  F  T  L
E  F  A  V  P  A  R  T  I  D  O
P  P  S  S  F  O  Y  B  E  L  A
O  A  D  B  Q  V  A  O  S  O  T
R  V  B  F  A  U  B  L  T  I  E
T  O  D  Y  S  T  E  A  A  B  N
E  I  A  E  F  I  I  T  L  P  I
S  L  T  S  I  L  S  E  B  T  S
P  R  P  F  U  T  B  O  L  O  S
A  V  O  L  I  B  O  L  U  E  L
M  U  S  E  O  T  L  O  F  M  U
```

G Working in pairs, draw and cut out pictures showing a soccer ball, a beach ball, a balloon and a painting. While one of you points to each picture cue and asks "Where are you going?" in Spanish, the other responds in Spanish.

EJEMPLO:

A: ¿Adónde vas tú?

B: Voy a la playa.

H Interview five of your classmates to find out what they like to do in their free time. Ask each student the questions that follow and record each answer (*sí* or *no*) in the space provided on this sheet. Then summarize your findings.

	Student 1	Student 2	Student 3	Student 4	Student 5
1. ¿Te gusta nadar?	_____	_____	_____	_____	_____
2. ¿Te gusta bailar?	_____	_____	_____	_____	_____
3. ¿Te gusta leer?	_____	_____	_____	_____	_____
4. ¿Te gusta montar a caballo?	_____	_____	_____	_____	_____
5. ¿Te gusta montar en bicicleta?	_____	_____	_____	_____	_____
6. ¿Te gusta esquiar?	_____	_____	_____	_____	_____
7. ¿Te gusta el fútbol?	_____	_____	_____	_____	_____
8. ¿Te gusta el béisbol?	_____	_____	_____	_____	_____

Every major Latin American newspaper has a review of various local, national and international sporting events. Look at the following sports summary *(sumario deportivo)* and then answer the questions that follow. Here are some words that you may need to know:

se cumplirá = will take place   **viajaron** = they traveled

equitadores = equestrians   **juez** = judge

deportistas = athletes   **voleibol** = volibol

interempresas = corporate

SUMARIO DEPORTIVO

COPA CARTIER DE POLO.- Por lo menos diez equipos participarán en la tercera Copa Cartier de Polo, que se cumplirá entre el 15 de julio y el 1 de agosto, en las instalaciones del Polo Club de Bogotá. Entre los conjuntos se destacan el García-Arriba, que representa al club Campestre de Cali, reforzado con el jugador argentino Fortunato Gómez, y, El Silencio, cuya principal figura es Santiago Gastambide, con ocho goles de handicap.

CIRCUITO BRETAÑA DE TENIS.- Sin contratiempos para las siembras principales, se cumplieron los partidos de la fase de octavos de final en la quinta parada del circuito Bretaña prejuvenil de tenis en el club del Comercio de Pereira. En masculino, en las dos categorías, Bogotá y Antioquia clasificaron a cuartos el mayor número de jugadores por Liga, cuatro cada uno. También avanzaron representantes de Valle (2), Santander (2), Quindío (2), Risaralda (2) y Cauca (1).

EQUITADORES EN QUITO.- Viajaron a Quito cinco jinetes colombianos (tres juveniles y dos infantiles) para competir en el concurso ecuestre internacional de salto "Valorfinsa", que se realiza entre viernes y domingo en el Quito Tennis Club. Se trata de los juveniles Eric Terwengel (Bogotá), John Pérez (Bogotá) y Juan M. García (Cali) y de los infantiles Hernando Forero L. (Bogotá) y Natalia Ballen (Medellín), bajo la dirección técnica de Alvaro Posada C. La actividad ecuestre también seguirá en el país con pruebas de adiestramiento en Bogotá y Cali.

CAFAM, CAMPEON INTEREMPRESAS.- La Caja de Compensación Familiar-Cafam ganó el título general del torneo interempresas, con triunfos en tejo, natación y baloncesto. En total fueron ocho las disciplinas en competencia, con participación de 3.000 deportistas de 320 empresas de la capital colombiana. Ahora se anuncian inscripciones para el torneo del segundo semestre, en la sede de Cafam de la Floresta. Estarán abiertas hasta el 23 de julio, en baloncesto, fútbol, microfútbol y tejo.

PRESELECCION DE VOLEIBOL.- La comisión técnica de la Federación Colombiana de Voleibol convocó a 18 jugadoras para el XX Campeonato Suramericano de voleibol, categoría mayores, que se disputará en El Cuzco, Perú, entre el 12 y 19 de septiembre, con participación de equipos de Brasil, Argentina, Chile, Perú, Paraguay, Venezuela y Colombia. Las jugadoras preseleccionadas son, Antioquia: Silvia Jaramillo, Claudia Lebrún, Mónica Fernández, Erika Alvarez, Marisol Mosquera, Gloria Peláez y Mónica Ramírez. Bogotá: Crisberth Gómez, Glinnys Valencia, Sandra Cano, María Constanza Blanco, Gloria María González, Mónica Duque y Carol Flórez. Valle: Isabel Silva, Natalia García, Claudia Lorena de la Cruz y Margarita Vargas. El técnico es el cubano Jorge Surená.

GRANDES LIGAS.- Los siguientes fueron los resultados de los partidos de las Grandes Ligas de béisbol, jugados el viernes por la noche. Liga Nacional: Florida 4, Filadelfia 3. Montreal 8, Atlanta 2. San Diego 6, Colorado 3 (primer partido). San Diego 6, Colorado 2 (segundo partido). Chicago 6, St. Louis 4. Los Angeles 3, Cincinnati 2. San Francisco 4, Houston 3. Liga Americana: Detroit 5, Boston 1. Toronto 11, Milwaukee 10 (11 entradas). Baltimore 8, Cleveland 1. Minnesota 4, N. York 3. California 7, Chicago 3. Texas 5, Seattle 3. Oakland 5, Kansas City 2.

RALLYE DE NUEVA ZELANDA.- El español Carlos Sainz se adjudicó ayer siete de los once tramos especiales de la tercera etapa del Rallye de Nueva Zelanda y fue, con diferencia, el piloto más rápido de la jornada, lo que le permitió recortar en medio minuto la desventaja con sus predecesores a falta de un día para la conclusión de la prueba.

JUEZ INTERNACIONAL.- El juez de boxeo profesional Milton Mercado se desplazará este miércoles a Lanusse, Argentina, para actuar como juez de la contienda mundialista de la categoría welter junior entre el argentino Juan Martín Coggi y el venezolano José Barbosa, combate que se cumplirá el viernes 13 de agosto. Mercado es oriundo de Barranquilla.

1. When is the polo cup going to take place?

   _____

2. At what club did the tennis match take place?

   _____

3. To what city did the equestrians travel?

   _____

4. How many athletes participated in the corporate tournament?

   _____

5. Which South American countries will participate in the 20th annual volleyball championship?

   _____

6. Who won the baseball game between Oakland and Kansas City?

   _____

7. What country hosted a rally?

   _____

8. What sport does Milton Mercado judge?

   _____

Unit 19

A Which item in each group costs the most? Circle the letter of the item that generally is the most expensive.

1. a. una regla   b. un abrigo   c. tres duraznos

2. a. un cuaderno   b. un vaso de leche   c. un CD

3. a. una silla   b. cinco tomates   c. un bolígrafo

4. a. un lápiz   b. una camisa   c. unos calcetines

5. a. unos tenis   b. un café   c. unas zapatillas

6. a. unas habichuelas   b. un tomate   c. cien duraznos

B Complete each sentence by changing each English word in parentheses to its corresponding Spanish word.

1. (peaches)   Voy a comprar unos _____ .

2. (how much)   ¿ _____ cuesta este CD?

3. (looking)   Estoy _____ , nada más.

4. (all)   Eso es _____ .

5. (change)   Aquí esta el _____ .

C Circle the letter of the most appropriate answer to each question.

1. ¿Adónde vas tú?

   a. Lo compro.

   b. Unos tenis.

   c. Al mercado.

2. ¿Cuánto cuesta este CD?

   a. Cuesta 25,00 pesos.

   b. Estoy mirando, nada más.

   c. Aquí está el dinero.

3. ¿Algo más?

   a. ¡Es un poco caro!

   b. Aquí está el cambio.

   c. Pues, unas habichuelas.

4. ¿En que puedo servirle?

   a. Al centro comercial.

   b. Estoy mirando, nada más. Gracias.

   c. Es un cliente.

5. ¿Qué vas a comprar?

   a. Unos zapatos.

   b. Unas ofertas.

   c. Un vendedor.

6. ¿Cuesta este pantalón 15,00 pesos?

   a. Aquí están las monedas.

   b. Sí, es una oferta.

   c. Muchas gracias.

D Complete these mini-dialogues with the appropriate words.

1. **A:** ¿En qué puedo _____ ?

   B: _____ mirando, nada más. Gracias.

2. **A:** ¿Qué vas a _____ ?

   B: _____ tenis.

3. **A:** ¿_____ caro el chocolate?

   B: No, es muy _____ .

4. **A:** ¿_____ vas tú?

   B: Voy al centro _____ .

5. **A:** ¿Algo _____ ?

   B: _____ , diez duraznos, por favor.

E

I. The conversation that follows is between a salesclerk and a customer, but the sentences are all mixed up. Rearrange them by putting them in logical order, beginning with "1" for the first sentence in the dialogue, "2" for the second sentence, etc. Number 1 is already marked for you.

__1__ ¿En qué puedo servirle?

_____ Gracias. ¿Algo más?

_____ ¿Cuánto cuesta este CD?

_____ Está bien. Lo compro. Aquí está el dinero.

_____ Cuesta 29,00 pesos.

_____ No, eso es todo.

II. Now, in the space below, copy all the sentences in their correct order.

_____

_____

_____

_____

_____

F Find your way through the store to the cash register. Name the items you encounter on
your way.

_____   _____

_____   _____

_____   _____

_____

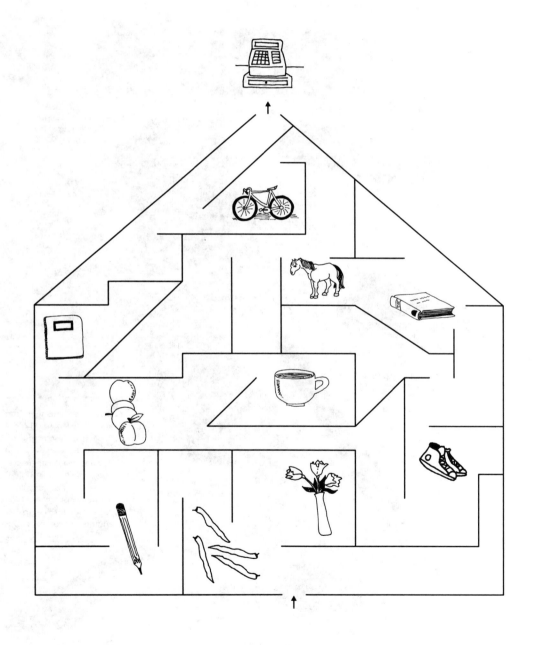

G Imagine you are shopping at El Corte Inglés, a famous department store in Spain. Answer the questions that follow *en español*. Remember that the monetary unit in Spain is the peseta. Here are some words that you may need to know:

cuestan = they cost

piso de goma = rubber sole

bolso = purse

pendientes = earrings

BURBERRYS
Abrigo cruzado de lana, 102.965
Traje de chaqueta de ojo de perdiz con cuello de terciopelo, 47.895
Blusa lisa, 16.990

El Corte Inglés

VERÓNICA
Pendientes de plata chapada de 1ª ley y circonitas, 9.775

LLANERO
Cinturones de piel sport-ciudad, 4.250

Camisas de manga larga estampada, viscosa 100%
1 camisa, 4.750
2 camisas, 8.500

Bolígrafo Expert, 7.800

VELILLA
Zapato de nobuk y piso de goma con cordones, tallas 23 a 33, tallas 24 a 26, 4.895

ANDREU
Corbatas de gran diseño en ambiente de colorido pastel, 2.500

1. Zapatos de ante negro con adorno de fantasía, 12.950
2. Zapatos de raso negro con adorno de fantasía, 12.950
3. Zapatos de raso negro con adorno de fantasía, 12.950
4. Zapatos de raso negro con adorno de pedrería, 11.950
5. Zapatos de raso negro con adorno de pedrería, 12.950

CORALINA
Suéter largo de lana-angora, 12.900

Bolso de fiesta en metal dorado, 6.950

1. ¿Cuánto cuesta el cinturón de piel?

    _____

2. ¿Cuánto cuestan las corbatas?

    _____

3. ¿Cuánto cuestan los zapatos con piso de goma?

    _____

4. ¿Cuánto cuestan dos camisas de manga larga?

    _____

5. ¿Es el suéter de lana más caro que el bolígrafo?

    _____

6. ¿Es el abrigo más barato que los pendientes?

    _____

7. ¿Es el bolso de fiesta más caro que la corbata?

    _____

8. ¿Qué vas a comprar en El Corte Inglés?

    _____

    _____

Imagine that you're at a shopping center. You and your partner play the roles of a salesclerk and a customer. Carry on a short conversation in Spanish in which the customer makes a purchase. Limit your questions to those you have already practiced in class and be sure to respond appropriately to your partner's questions and comments. In the course of your conversation:

1) The clerk and the customer greet each other.

2) The clerk asks the customer if he or she wants some help.

3) The customer says what he or she wants to buy and asks the price of something.

4) The clerk tells the price.

5) The customer says that he or she will buy it.

6) The clerk asks if the customer wants anything else.

7) The customer says that's all and pays for the item.

8) The clerk thanks the customer and gives him or her change.

Unit 20

A Answer each travel question by circling the letter of the best answer.

1. Who carries a suitcase?

   a. una maleta   b. un viajero   c. un cliente

2. What tells you arrival and departure times?

   a. un pasaporte   b. un boleto   c. un horario

3. What permits you to travel internationally?

   a. un pasaporte   b. una maleta   c. una puerta

4. How can you get to Mérida?

   a. medianoche   b. en carro   c. el empleado

5. Which words tell you where something is?

   a. el siguiente tren   b. a las dos   c. a la derecha

B Complete each sentence with the most appropriate word in Spanish.

1. ¿A qué hora sale el _____ tren para Madrid?

2. Aquí está el _____ de ida y vuelta.

3. Bájese Ud. en la oficina de _____ .

4. ¿Cómo puedo _____ al hotel Ritz?

5. En la _____ 20.

C Find the best answer in column B to each question in column A.

A		B
1. ¿Dónde abordamos nosotros? _____		a. un boleto
2. ¿Qué compras? _____		b. a las nueve
3. ¿Cómo se llama el hotel? _____		c. en mi maleta
4. ¿A qué hora sale el autobús? _____		d. en la puerta 10
5. ¿Dónde está el pasaporte? _____		e. el Ritz

D I. Give the Spanish name for the means of transportation associated with each of the following words.

1. aeropuerto _____

2. estación del tren _____

3. océano _____

4. garaje _____

5. transporte público _____

II. Now write in Spanish that you are traveling by each of these means of transportation.

1. _____

2. _____

3. _____

4. _____

5. _____

E Complete each sentence with a word from the box.

vuelta	**avión**	**abordamos**
mostrador	*aeropuerto*	pasaportes

1. Viajo en el taxi al _____ .

2. Viajo en _____ a Caracas a las diez.

3. Me gustaría comprar un boleto de ida y _____ .

4. Voy a comprar el boleto en el _____ .

5. ¿Dónde está el control de _____ ?

6. ¿Dónde _____ nosotros?

F Descifra las palabras.

1. OROIHAR _____

2. RABOC _____

3. LACES _____

4. OTBELO _____

5. ROODTMSRA _____

6. RJAVIEO _____

7. ADLPMEEA _____

8. ONVIA _____

9. ALMAET _____

10. RAUTEP _____

G Imagine you are traveling by train to various cities in Spain and the following is your ticket for one trip. Look at the train ticket and answer the questions that follow. Here are some words that you may need to know:

billete = boleto

de = from

sello de emisión = stamp of issue

salida = departure

llegada = arrival

departamento = section

fuma = smoke

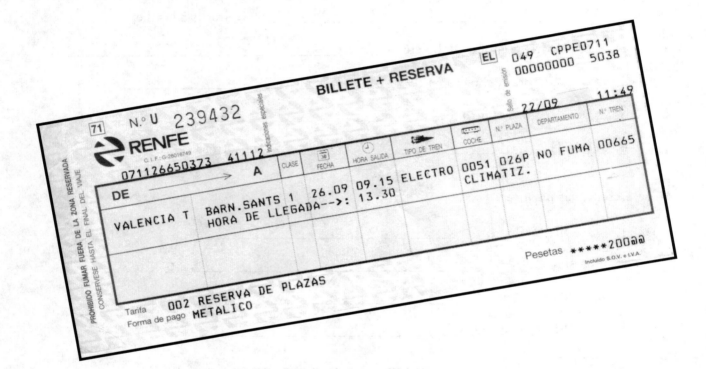

1. From what city are you departing?

   _____

2. On what date are you traveling?

   _____

3. On what date did you buy your ticket?

   _____

4. Do you have a first- or second-class ticket?

   _____

5. At what time does your train leave?

   _____

6. At what time does the train arrive at its destination?

   _____

7. Are you traveling in a smoking or a nonsmoking section?

   _____

8. What is the number of your train?

   _____

9. How much did your ticket cost?

   _____

Imagine that you're in a Spanish train station. You and your partner play the roles of a clerk at the ticket counter and a traveler. Carry on a short conversation in Spanish in which the traveler buys a train ticket. Limit your questions to those you have already practiced in class and be sure to respond appropriately to your partner's questions and comments. In the course of your conversation:

1) The clerk and the traveler greet each other.

2) The traveler tells the clerk what city he or she is going to and asks at what time the next train for that city is leaving.

3) The clerk tells the traveler the time.

4) The traveler tells the clerk that he or she wants a round-trip ticket in second class and asks the price.

5) The clerk tells the traveler the price.

6) The traveler pays for the ticket.

7) The clerk thanks the traveler and gives him or her change.